DELIBERATE ECONOMICS

A PATH TO FREEDOM FROM WAGE SLAVERY

ALEX ZIEBA, PhD

Seeley's Bay, Ontario, Canada

V 1.041720

ISBN: 9798616482426

Contents

CONTENTS

A note on the text, for Philosophers and other academic minds:

My perspective comes from life in Canada, heavily influenced by the evolution of market capitalism in the United States, which largely determined the character of our global economy.

Currencies are in Canadian or US dollars as stated in the text. These numbers are used to demonstrate qualitative relationships that hold regardless of currencies used, and will be slightly different in each Province or State, or in Europe, owing to differences in their minimum or average wages, currencies, and how the price of gold is calculated over time.

In order to present Deliberate Economics most clearly, I have avoided too many citations or footnotes. I feared complications would overshadow my purpose, which is to present a capitalist's critique of capitalism.

I first read H.D. Thoreau's _Walden_ (1854) by candlelight in my cabin. The reasons why it was recommended as relevant to my thesis were obvious: I needed a name for what I was proposing, and his coinage of a "deliberate life" allowed me to "situate it in the literature", as we are required to do to in dissertations. Thoreau believed that American lIfe already failed to bring felicity c1850, and conducted a lifestyle experiment in order to test this alternative. For a little over 2 years, he lived in a one room cabin he built, grew his own food and cut wood for heat, while selling some produce for cash, and later wrote _Walden_ as a journal of this experiment. Today, Thoreau's readers tend to rhapsodize nature and eulogize a simple life, or remember his civil disobedience, such as refusing to eat the food and wear the cotton produced by plantation slaves, or his refusal to pay taxes to an immoral state, which landed him in jail. To me, the few pages of accounting, the bottom line, was the point of the experiment. The transcendental consequences then follow.

Introduction: A Good Life

This book is for anyone worried about a future of low wages and environmental crises. Although based, like capitalism, on self-interest and the pursuit of profit, chances are that Business won't like it. Deliberate Economics shows how market capitalism consumes people's wages and causes environmental crises, revealing an easier and more certain alternative to meeting one's needs. If many shift their lifestyle in this direction, Deliberate Economics becomes the hidden key to what economists call *De-Growth*: finding profit in efficiencies that shrink the economy. Just as environmental degradation is a side effect of market capitalism, protecting our health, happiness and resources is a side effect of pursuing profit Deliberately.

In market capitalism, workers trade labour hours for wages, and then trade wages for commodities they need, like food, heat, and housing. Originally, this method of organizing society's labour was called *wage slavery,* in contrast to plantation slavery or feudal serfdom. Wage slavery is highly abstract: it is a shell game taken to social extremes, where one loses track of where the value of their wages went, instead of the nut. The best way to win a shell game is not play.

Deliberate Economics shows that we retain more value from our work— more profit— if we limit dependence on the market economy instead of trying to earn enough money as wage slaves to fulfill needs within it. To do something Deliberately means that the object of your labour is the object of your intention. That sounds abstract, but it's not. It means that you get food by growing it, you get a house by building it, and so on: you organize your own labour. Access to technologies means this is not a step back in time to the struggles of early homesteaders. Most would start on a Deliberate path in the city like I did, although some people live on land already. While you will still depend on the market economy for things like tools or property taxes, cutting the cost of necessities like food and housing increases the value of the cash you come by, by letting you apply all of it somewhere else, or save it until you need it.

Part 1 presents market capitalism from two perspectives. One is the perspective of Business Owners. The other is wage slaves, who are today called *workers, employees* or *Human Resources*. The relationship between masters and slaves is antagonistic in being designed for profit from slaves' labour and to keep wage slaves in their class. By applying Business-accounting principles to their job as if it were a business, wage slaves can see that the value of their labour is taken from them by design, through wage deflation, control over the money supply, and asset inflation. This reveals the value of producing Deliberately, in order to buy one's own freedom. I share the accounting from my 12-year Deliberate-life experiment. I was in a better financial position making $12 000 as a subsistence farmer doing renovations on the side than I could have been making $50 000 as a University Professor over those same years. A subsequent 12 years as a Professor making $80 000 confirms this finding. This shows that the vast majority of wage slave agreements—jobs—lose an opportunity cost comparison with a Deliberate approach. From a Business perspective, that means you shouldn't do it. Market Capitalism stops being a rational way to organize society when market players, the people, stop pursuing efficiency and stop pursuing their individual, rational self-interest.

Part 2 completes the picture of value extraction from wage slaves through consumer conveniences, and shares what I learned about saving labour while acquiring common necessities deliberately. First is a discussion of conveniences like processed food and credit cards; next, soap and laundry issues; and finally, growing food without digging soil, the Forest Way.

Part 3 is a discussion of where we have arrived, considering the extent to which different perspectives, such as age and economic position, affect the desirability of a Deliberate Life.

Rather than conclude by summarizing an essay, I share how I came to see wage slave and Business perspectives as inverted reflections of each other, and discover Deliberate Economics as a path to freedom from wage slavery.

Part 1: Market Capitalism from a Wage-Slave Perspective

Media discusses the economy from a Business perspective, as do most economists. Business textbooks do the same, explaining how Business Owners make money but not how their economic growth affects a wage slave. Understanding a wage-slave perspective sometimes means using different language for the same concepts. When we see a picture reflected in a mirror, the reflection is reversed, right is left and left is right: what Business calls inflation is deflation, what Business calls asset growth is our loss, what Business calls economic freedom is our oppression. This explains why people work so hard, and—despite the economic growth resulting from social cooperation, scale, and technology—struggle to survive. Deliberate Economics shows us a path to freedom from wage slavery.

1.1 Historical Development of Wage Slavery

Business talks about market capitalism as an expression of individual freedom. From the perspective of a worker, their freedom is a form of slavery. Calling people with jobs *wage slaves* reflects the language that Business and academics used themselves while capitalism was replacing feudalism and plantation slavery. Workers still use the language of slavery privately in comparing themselves to workhorses or rats on a wheel, but in public we use gentler terms, such as Human Resources. We can pick up the slavery debate where it left off, to see why *plantation* slavery was abolished and replaced by *wage* slavery in North America.

The US Civil War (1861–65) was concerned about slavery, but not about black lives. If the Civil War had been about human dignity, there would have been no reason for a Civil Rights movement a century later, or for a Black Lives movement today. The North and the South had developed incompatible economies because of how they used slaves. While other causes are cited for the war, an *economic* conflict over slavery is nowhere denied.

We are the resolution.

The South used slaves in a plantation economy, similar to the way landed gentry used serfs in a European feudal economy. Plantation slaves lived off of the land, and laboured to satisfy their need for food and housing. They were forced by the whip to perform additional labour for their master, who profited by selling commodities produced by the slaves and the land. Money was a *class commodity,* which means slaves did not get any. They could not spend it because their social status was as property not people, like a workhorse or a tractor today. They remained on the plantation, tended by family or other slaves, when they became old or disabled.

The North had developed a manufacturing economy that required a city or town and *employed* wage slaves. Wages were paid in money. To obtain this money and sometimes a new way of life, people left behind land they might have had, and their children were born into urban life. In the city they would have to meet their need for food and housing with wages, which transformed these needs into the necessity of a job. They sought out a slavemaster instead of the slavemaster seeking them, which made their servitude appear to be a mutually beneficial agreement, as a product of their free choice rather than a product of the whip. Once they became old or disabled, they were sent out the door.

There were of course debates about which was the more profitable form of economy, and even which was more humane. The language made clear that this was a choice between types of slavery. Both were capitalist economies and perceived an essential need to trade, without which they may have agreed to disagree, and just left each other alone.

The problem was that one system allowed slaves to use money and the other didn't. Their different ways of organizing production and distribution meant they couldn't join the Northern and Southern economies and determine the value of a US dollar, or the market value of a commodity. They would have to merge their economies to trade. Paying wages would undermine the plantation economy, and giving wage slaves land and seasonal time to grow their own food would undermine the manufacturing economy. War settled the debate. The South sang nostalgic about their lost economic freedom, and the North spun Disneyesque stories about slavery being wrong—and wage slavery became the norm.

When I talk about a Deliberate path to freedom, it is freedom from wage slavery, being free from this *necessity* of a job. Our animal nature makes labour necessary to survive, but the exercise of social power to accomplish the will of a few, in order to satisfy our nature, is the oppression of wage slavery.

Note the insight that we can draw about conflicts with socialist economies—even if their socialism was the product of their free democratic election, as with the unprovoked US attack on Chile in 1973. Why not agree to disagree? Just as the South saw wage slavery undermining their economic freedom, market capitalism presents its barrier to trade with socialist economies as an attack on our way of life, wherein "freedom" is at stake. Academics similarly argued during the Cold War about which form of oppression was more efficient, and which was more humane. These debates had no bearing on military decisions. The date of the attack on Chile, on Tuesday, September 11, acquired ideological significance in the choice of date and target of the attack on the World Trade Centre in 2001. An attack on freedom, we said.

While in an ordinary sense capital is money invested, at the same time, *Capital is social power*. It is social power because a person with capital has the power to tell other people what to do, in proportion to the amount of capital they exercise. If you find yourself with some cash and go out for dinner, you exercise just so much social power in spending the cash, in the sense that someone else cooked your meal and brought it to your table; the cook and waiter are responding to their necessity for a job. If they provide good service, you'll pay a little more, a tip, for hiding the resentment you know is there, although this is not always expected. Either way, if they want to get paid, they submit their will to your capital, your social power.

Investing capital in a Business similarly means organizing workers' lives in exchange for wages, but exercising capital for profit, rather than for consumption as above, is the investor's Busy-ness. The cook and waiter were caught between the customer's capital and the restaurant Owner's capital.

Capital is therefore the medium of oppression. Because the necessity for a job brings the wage slaves' compliance, and capital buys freedom from this necessity, there is no other way to appropriate the social power being exercised over a wage slave than through capital. In other words, wage slaves, like Business Owners, have to buy their freedom.

While wage slaves are permitted to use money and buy their freedom, the structure of society and the function of capital mean few will be able to do so. And so we turn next to the socio-economic structure of market capitalism.

Market capitalism consists of 2 economic classes, Business Owners and wage slaves, along with an intermediate set of Owner-Operators.

The Business Owners are those who own the means of production and distribution—the factories, retail outlets, businesses that people work for, landlords collecting rent, truck and ship fleets, etc. Because they own these forms of capital, they meet their own need for money by profiting from the organization of wage slaves, or by trading capital between themselves, which is the exercise and trading of social power.

Once wealthy enough they hire executives to manage their investments, who exercise this power on their behalf. Today we refer to the wealthiest of these as "The 1%", and believe that 8 men exercise half the world's capital.

Wage slaves make up the bulk of the population. They are distinguished by the fact that they have no access to the land or food needed for survival and neither do they have cash, and this necessitates making wage slave agreements, or crime. No capital, no social power. It is as if we were born stranded in someone's city or plantation, with no ancestral territory, no nation or tribe, so we belong nowhere and must negotiate our status with the Owners. A person who already has access to the resources for survival—in much of the world, that's a few acres of land, some treed and some farmable, with a water supply—can be much more choosy about what they do or don't do for money, but a resourceless person has to take whatever job is on offer. Risking health, engaging in activities that are socially or environmentally harmful, and ignoring corruption, are seen as normal, necessary evils.

Owner-operators are the self employed. They own their means of production and in this sense have some capital, but master their own labour rather than retain wage slaves. Owner-operators or family businesses are held up as a moral ideal, although they are rare in relation to the number of workers. Despite periodic resurgence in things like artisanal yogurt, home-made soap or goat wool, they are always threatened, because if their business is profitable, they must grow into full-fledged Business Owners themselves, or be pushed aside by them. As a result Owner-operators are not their own class. They exist only as a transitional set, representing people on a wedge between classes. Their skill may be replaced by a machine or computer, just as power looms made hand weaving obsolete; or their product may be legislated away, as the requirement for pasteurized milk has done to small dairy operations, or as prohibition and regulation have done to artisanal alcohol, tobacco, cannabis, and opium.

Nevertheless, escaping wage slavery requires owning some means of production, recovering social power, and so moves one into this transitional set.

Our relationship to the economy looks different from the perspective of wage-slaves than from the perspective of Business Owners. It is a fundamentally antagonistic relationship. Wage slaves' first want is the necessities of life, while Business Owners must obstruct wage slaves' path to these necessities with their Busy-ness, in order to profit and survive as a class.

1.2 The Middle-Class Chimera

We've been looking at the antagonism between Business Owners and wage slaves, as the primary socio-economic classes in capitalism today. Owner-Operators are rare, a transitional set rather than a class of their own. Today, there is no middle class.

"The middle class" was first uttered as a derogatory term, what we now call a micro-aggression. As capitalism replaced feudalism, Business Owners were called *the Bourgeoisie*, a French word for town-dwellers. They were also called the *middle* class, because they were a new social power rising up within feudalism. They were neither aristocrats nor serfs, but something new in the middle; they found an unexploited conceptual space in the feudal economy the French called *entre-preneurs*, or "between-takers". They lacked aristocratic manners, and in this sense were not "classy". So, the term *middle class* was doubly derogatory, carrying aristocratic resentment of economic loss, and insulting the social manners of those who took it.

'In the middle classes one is made constantly aware of shifting lines of demarcation. Mr. Vincy, the Mayor, a ribbon manufacturer, came of a Middlemarch family that had "kept a good house for three generations, in which there had been much intermarrying with neighbours more or less decidedly genteel." His sister Harriet had "made a wealthy match" in accepting the Banker Mr. Bulstrode, "who, however, as a man not born in the town, and altogether of dimly known origin, was considered to have done well in uniting himself with a real Middlemarch family." Mr. Vincy, on the other hand, was thought to have descended a little, having married an innkeeper's daughter. The Vincy children were sent to the best schools, Rosamond to Mrs. Lemon's, where she acquired enough superficial finish to be ashamed of her family's hearty bourgeois manners, and Fred to the University in vain hope he would advance his social standing by entering the Church. Rosamond is more like her family than she supposes in striving to elevate herself by marrying Lydgate, who is the son of a gentlemen and nephew of a baronet, though he has somewhat lowered himself by becoming a doctor.'

—G.S. Haight, quoting George Eliot's <u>Middlemarch</u> , 1872, in the introduction to the 1956 Riverside Edition.

Over time, Owner-operators, or the *Petty Bourgeoisie,* became subject to this insult in the language of socialists, who called wage slaves *the Proletariat*. Today, those who defend capitalism and aspire for material gain may be called bourgeois, but now the insult comes from wage slaves who might call *themselves* the middle class, and who also resent their economic loss, and in a different way, the manners of those who took it.

The only thing the middle class is not is the Royal Family. Because Business Owners, Owner Operators or even wage slaves can be "the middle class", it has lost any fixed reference. The micro-aggression is also ambiguous, because aspiring to the middle class is praiseworthy too—a sign of ambition. If "the middle class" can be anybody, good or bad, then it identifies nobody, like "people". In Canada, the new Minister of Middle Class Prosperity had to admit there is no way to define the middle class (Jan 28, 2020).

On this socio-economic view, there is no such thing as a middle class.

Nevertheless, the middle class is the target audience for most political speeches and marketing, now represented with a Ministry in the Canadian Government. The middle class lives only in people's minds.

The middle class is a chimera: a mythological demon with many faces, made up of the parts of different animals. This plasticity allows any who invoke it to paint the faces as they like. Imagination, fancy, delusion, are adaptable that way. The *middle-class chimera*, in which people see themselves reflected, is a vague image of someone with a job, housing, transportation, clothes, etc., and a story about this being better than what a poor person has. A participant. A team player. They are smiling, whether they are relaxing on a beach with strangers or at the local fast food outlet with friends. The chimera is at once an image of oneself and that which one aspires to become, even if this image is stretched, like Barbie's trademarked figure, to impossible proportions.

The middle-class chimera replaced the slavemaster's whip to control the wage slave's will. It holds a carrot on a claw at the end of one paw, and a stick in the other.

All cultures have their demons. These manifestations of fears and desires are dangerous supplements to the identities that we might have. The middle-class chimera is the demon of market capitalism. The social power of demons and delusions lies in their lack of material definition. They exist only at the site of their effect, the irrational things they make us do. It's like identifying black holes, as gravity sources that had to be there in order to account for the light disappearing, which is the value of our labour, and our planet. Identifying demons is the first step to slaying them.

Workers from minimum wage to 6-figure salaries are invited to think Politicians and Business are speaking to them through the Media, and to the extent that the audience has wage slavery and one vote in common, they are. Children are not excepted: the chimera says they *need* the running shoes worn by some celebrity, and parents want to make them happy, help them "fit-in". Like Barbie, and Ken. Identification with the middle-class chimera is nurtured along with our body as we learn young to shape our will to it.

1.3 Business, Government and Media

From a wage-slave perspective, market capitalism is based on an antagonistic relationship between two socio-economic classes, where capital is the social power through which Business organizes the lives of wage slaves. There is no middle class, except as it exists in people's minds, guiding their will.

The Media often presents this middle class with debates about whether Government or Business should take the lead on social or environmental problems. Sometimes papers propose Public-Private Partnerships for these purposes. And sometimes the Media will make us aware of an issue, after which we may demand Government take action against Business.
Just as this language assumes the middle class is the audience, real contracts and social policies resulting from these theatrics assume that Business, Government, and Media really are 3 independent, autonomous social powers.

But if we look closely, we find these are manifestations of the same social power, capital. Business, Government, and Media are controlled by the same *people*. Politicians are, for the most part, corporate lawyers and executives, or Owners who put their assets into a Trust during their tenure as Leaders. With few exceptions, Media are controlled by a handful of Corporations or funded by Government. Social Media remain the same as television and newspapers in earning revenue by selling their audience to other Businesses, as ad space. What is new in social media is that the audience produces content at its own expense, and in doing so, provides personal information to sell, allowing individually targeted advertising. For example, a message with "Trip to Cuba" in the subject line will result in travel ads in the corner of the screen when you check the weather later.

Business, Government and Media look like 3 independent and autonomous social powers, but the people in control are Business Owners, with a common Business perspective. On analogy, football players have a common perspective about what a goal looks like, even if they are competing on different teams. They have a common interest in keeping their league going over time, and agree that without fans in seats it is not possible to win games.

One of my first lessons in Business school was that if you don't want the Government making laws that reduce your profitability, then get elected and make the laws yourself.

We see this advice reflected in the sophistry of laws and policies that sound progressive while not interfering with Business. For example, the UN boasts "17 Sustainable Development Goals" that are the basis for international-development policy and project funding (or, how tax dollars get spent), but none of these goals is targeted at reducing carbon emissions. Goal 13, "Climate Action", is about *economically* sustainable farming and development, which means that one gets funding by being ready for droughts and floods that are coming, as long as one plans to expand AgriBusiness. The Paris Accord pretends to be an international agreement to reduce carbon emissions, but signatories did not agree to reduce carbon emissions. It says nothing about overpopulation, or minimizing global trade, or air travel, or the decline in atmospheric oxygen. If reducing carbon

20

is the goal, primary sources of carbon emissions should be topics, at least. Instead, the Paris Accord permits Governments to subsidize the development of an electric economy, without their trade partners complaining that these subsidies violate other trade agreements. Few people read trade agreements, whose Media summaries make it look like they pursue some other goal than profit, while Business is winning games as usual.

We often speak as though our Government were an institution for managing the common affairs of the people, rather than Business, and then complain about its failure to meet those expectations.

At the same time, most are aware that Business selects the candidates and puts up the money to run election campaigns. Candidates advertise their success in Business or their relationship to a wealthy family as reason for the middle class to believe they will be good Politicians. Rather than a Government formed by the people for the people, *a Government formed by Business Owners is a bureaucracy for managing the common interests and conflicts of Business Owners*. During the Civil War in the US and in British North America (later Canada), the eligibility to vote still depended on property ownership, making it clear that this Democracy was an arena for Business alone. Politicians may disagree about how best to do it, but agree that managing the economy is their purpose, their goal.

Where the purpose of a Business is to make a profit, the purpose of a Government formed through the cooperation of Business leaders is to maintain and promote the social conditions for profitability. These conditions include keeping wage slaves in their class, as consumers and a labour pool. This is reflected in the Media, particularly at election time, when Politicians make their Business conflicts public. Government fiddling with interest rates and unemployment rates looks to maintain unemployment (and therefore poverty) at a particular level, rather than solve it, because if there were no unemployment, then workers could demand better wages, and profitability would decline.

Wage slaves getting better pay is bad for Business Owners, but good for wage slaves. Perspective. Poverty and unemployment are maintained, on this view, because it is cheaper for Business as a class to pay a few people on welfare less than $2/hour not to work, than to allow wages to rise for all. It's no different than paying farmers not to farm, a common subsidy when overproduction of a commodity is driving prices down because Business wants to keep the cost of that commodity low. It's no accident that these commodities are wage slaves and their food. Maintaining a welfare class also provides wage slaves with something to point to, hate, and want to avoid, and so is an ideological incentive to work.

"Corruption" means doing something illegal. In its time, plantation slavery was legal. There is no corruption described here. Everything is legal, and makes sense from a Business perspective.

Perhaps the starkest contrast between Business Owner and wage-slave perspectives comes when we evaluate good and bad through Gross National Product, or GDP.

> GDP =
> *Private consumption*
> *+ gross investment*
> *+ government investment*
> *+ government spending*
> *+ (exports - imports).*

We hear about it all the time. If GDP is up, that's good for *the* economy and good for "us", and when it's down that's bad; if it is down for a while that's a "recession", and after that a "depression", and these things are bad for "us", so the story goes. It makes sense to Business Owners', who are the "we" and the "us", talking to each other about *their* economy through their Media. GDP excludes all Deliberate production or unpaid domestic labour, re-sold used or re-purposed products; it vilifies the free market as a "black market", and makes no account of externalities like pollution or the well being of people in general. Because all of this is excluded, GDP recognizes only revenue in the Business Owners' economy. This results in perverse judgments about "good" and "bad", if we think they were talking about us.

Any time the Government spends money or a Business Owners' product or service is purchased, GDP goes up. So, if your home is robbed, vandalized or damaged by a storm, that's *good* for their economy. If you need a $1million cancer treatment, that's *good* for their economy. Lose all your money at the casino: *good*. War is *good:* you need to replace arms as well as what they destroyed. Buying anything is *good*, but buying it at the regular price, instead of half price, is exactly *twice as good*. Eat imported food on disposable dishes: *good*; local food on plates you washed: *bad*.

By contrast, unemployment peaked at about 25% during the Great Depression, and has been below 10% since. During recessions, everything from surplus products to houses and stocks goes on sale, temporarily increasing the value of wages for the 90%+ who still have them. Good. If we moderate our consumption, stay out of debt and stay healthy, GDP goes down and that's bad for the Business Owners' economy, bad for "us", but good for wage slaves whose finances and health are now in order. Really good.

From the perspective of a wage slave evaluating GDP, we can start to see why capital, which drives Business and Government, is *incapable* of addressing poverty or environmental degradation. While at first glance to do so is bad for Business, they are incapable because their social power is capital, derived from investment that exists to make a profit. Owners entrust a Board of Directors with the responsibility of seeking profit on their behalf. When these Owners and their Executives are cooperating as a Government, enhancing the social conditions for profitability is the responsibility entrusted to Politicians. Therefore, capital, the social lever at their disposal, is a power to grow GDP and generate profit, in an economy that creates poverty and environmental problems as it grows.

Capital, or Business and Politicians, are not able to achieve any other kind of value than profit, unless they can contrive these other kinds of value as an accidental consequence of profit seeking. By analogy, if you have a well-drilling rig, you have the power to drill holes. When the problem is that old holes need to be filled in, there is nothing you can do about it, even if you want to, except drill new holes next to them and hope some of the debris falls in—but then you made new holes.

POPULAR MECHANICS  341

The furnaces of the world are now burning about 2,000,000,000 tons of coal a year. When this is burned, uniting with oxygen, it adds about 7,000,000,000 tons of carbon dioxide to the atmosphere yearly. This tends to make the air a more effective blanket for the earth and to raise its temperature. The effect may be considerable in a few centuries.

— Francis Molena, The Remarkable Weather of 1911. March 1912

Carbon-offset schemes work this way, pretending to use profit for good instead of bad. For example, a coffee seller finances a tree-farming business by charging *extra*, claiming to offset the carbon emissions from imported coffee in disposable cups (first hole) based on estimates of how fast the trees grow. When the trees are industrially mature, the plan is to cut them down and release their carbon in another production cycle, rather than protect them for several centuries to fill the first hole as the consumer believed. When they harvest the trees, we have two holes to fill: one from the imported coffee in disposable cups, and one from the harvested trees. They have the profit

24

generated by digging both. This accounting ignores that the field for the tree farm had been a forest before it was cleared for farming, an existing third hole, because then we would realize that playing this shell game doubled our emissions without addressing the issue of the past. Placated consumers provided *extra* operating capital for the forest-products sector, while increasing GDP and carbon emissions. The Paris Accord fully approves of carbon-trading schemes.

Most wage slaves know that they are a rat on a wheel struggling to meet their needs against unseen forces, and are interested in practical solutions. If Government and Business are the same people, and are incapable of addressing problems caused by *their* economic growth, that leaves wage slaves, the bulk of the population, or no one.

Limits to resources and market growth potential mean that we cannot continue to rely on constant growth, or more profit and more GDP, for our economy to function. This reality is part of a young person's anxiety today.

Since growth is the cause, some economists propose "De-Growth", the opposite of "growth", which requires that we find profit in shrinking global GDP. This appears contradictory from a Business perspective, because Business sees growth as the only path to profit. A wage-slave perspective shows that Deliberate Economics is the key to de-growth, but that's getting ahead a bit. Conceptually, Deliberate Economics sees this idea of *making* work or *making* jobs as the Busy-ness absurdity that it is, where Owners contrive story plots and images that make jobs, increase consumption, and increase GDP.

From the perspective of an ordinary person trying to live, completing all of your work and having time for family, friends, leisure, is not a problem to complain about or correct, not bad for you, not bad for us: instead, finishing work is the whole point. Good for you. Good for us.

1.4 Declining Value of Wages

We have been looking at market capitalism from the perspective of a wage slave, based on an antagonistic relationship with Business Owners, whose social power, capital, is exercised for the purpose of growing GDP in order to profit. On this view, there is no such thing as a middle class any longer, although the middle-class chimera is the whip that shapes fears and desires to gain our complicity to work and spend and work again, as Business desires.

Better-paid workers and corporate executives are still wage slaves. In theory, the better pay is required to obtain their willingness to manage complicated or onerous tasks. Ford's iconic decision to pay workers twice the average rate was based on this thinking, because Ford had trouble retaining workers, making training costs and production halts more expensive than paying them double the average wage. A Ford assembly line worker could buy a Model-T with 4 months' wages, but it would take them 3 years to get an F-150 today.

Better pay, in any job, is threatened by market conditions, as once there are more workers available, maybe in another country, they will do the same job for lower wages. And there was only one Ford, which is to say, there are a limited number of blossoming market sectors that can afford high wages. Once those positions are filled, the rest of us must take whatever job we can get.

Remember we are comparing what we can do in a day today with what else we can do in a day today, so improvements in the standard of technology our labour is applied to were constant. Based on a first-hand account, "Between [1910] and 1914 the car became quite common, mostly Model T Fords. This was a friction driven car propelled by a motor with magneto ignition, no water pump, and the water circulated when it got warm enough. The connecting rods had paddles that splashed oil up into the cylinder walls. The result was — that when you were going uphill — your number four spark plug fouled; and when you were going downhill, your number one cylinder got most of the oil. Consequently you seldom had all four cylinders operating at the same time. The lights on the first models were carbide lamps that were about on a par with two fireflies. These were followed by lights that were powered by current from the magneto, which lights were fair when operating at, or near, top speed, which was 38 or 40 mph. However, these lights were mostly non-existent when you slowed down for bad roads, which was most of the time. The Model T didn't have much to recommend it by today's standards except for the fact that it was cheap ($500) with all accessories, including a screw driver and a set of pliers. AND it never wore out."
— Everett John Elliott, The Way it Used to Be, 1977

This decline in the value of wages is a consequence of a competitive job market in which wage slaves are traded. Like any commodity, the price of Human Resources settles around production cost, or the level required for wage slaves to be fed, housed, clothed, educated, etc., so they can show up for work again the next day. The money, wages, goes back to Business Owners—when you pay for food, housing, clothes, taxes— who, as a class, provided the wages to start with. It may seem counterintuitive: why should an employer that makes cars feel good about you giving your wages to another who serves fast food? We'll get to consumer conveniences in Part 2. Recognize for now how competition amongst wage slaves for the same job drives down the average wage for all. If the job is complicated, a bunch of youth will go to school for it because they heard it pays well, and then get out of school and find that competition, from so many more qualified graduates, brings lower-than-expected wages to the entire sector, as well as student debt.

At the bottom of the competition is the planet, or "natural resources". These have zero value in the Business Owners' economy—no number entered in the books. Let's say that you cut firewood to sell. You price your wood to pay your costs and time, and, hypothetically, include a cost for the tree itself, for the resource. There is a conceptual problem in assigning a price for the tree here: there is no reason to see why you should get that extra cash, or what the tree stump who literally produced the wood would do with it, which is why the stump never gets it. Sort of like a plantation slave.... It doesn't matter. Quickly, one who is out of work but also has access to trees will sell for less, declaring trees as free for the taking, like fish in the sea, and you will have to do the same to compete. Hence the price of resources in Business Owners' accounting only reflects their cost to remove them; like Human Resources, natural resources are considered worthless beyond production cost, or the money spent. There is no accounting, literally, for the lost old-growth forests, the depleted topsoil, the herds of caribou and buffalo, the schools of fish that could stop a ship in its tracks, or the decline in atmospheric oxygen (air is free).

Business Owners' drive to reduce the cost of wage slaves results in more profit, so is good from their perspective. The value of wages fell by more than half since the mid-1960s. While my experience is in Canada, the pattern is similar throughout market capitalism.

From a wage-slave perspective, the mid-1960's was the peak of market capitalism because it provided a higher standard of living to slaves than at any time in human history. Politics at the time rallied around John Rawls' <u>Theory of Justice</u>, that because our poorest people were better off than the poorest in any other regime, our form of social cooperation was morally superior. This argument made the chimera's tendency to cause social and environmental problems a fair concession in exchange for that better life for slaves. By "better", they meant better than some other kind of social oppression, like mass starvation in Ethiopia, or the Socialism of the USSR, or something from history like plantation slavery.

Usually, people expect the results of cooperating to be "better" than they could do on their own. Deliberate Economics uses this more intuitive comparison. A similarly intuitive argument defending wage slavery during the same period was the Social Pie argument. The Social Pie argument says that if wage slaves cooperate to make a Social Pie rather than make their own pies, then even though their share as a percentage of the Pie goes down, their individual slice of the bigger Social Pie still grows larger absolutely. This presents wage slavery as profitable for the slave. For example, 100% of a $6000 pie is $6000, but 10% of a $100 000 pie is $10 000. On the basis of an opportunity-cost comparison, it is *possible* for me to be better off getting a fraction of something large compared to all of something small. In theory, social cooperation is more profitable because of the division of labour and scale, augmented by technology.

Comparing advantage this way, it might have been true in the mid-1960s that one was better able to satisfy their needs for food and housing as a wage slave than Deliberately. It is no longer true. The Social Pie argument requires that wage slaves get more pie per person as the pie grows. We no longer hear about the Social Pie argument because it shows that our individual slice of pie gets smaller as the pie grows, *despite* all of the advantages of social cooperation and scale, augmented by technology.

At that time—forgive the sexism, there have been changes to our middle-class chimera since—so I'll say in 1965, a man working 40 hours a week could support a "middle-class" lifestyle. He could pay for housing, a car, support a wife at home who performs unpaid domestic work, 3.5 kids (this was the Baby Boom) with their own rooms and needs fulfilled, running water, TV, a pension, maybe an annual vacation. In the TV series *All in the Family* (1971ff), even blue-collar worker Archie Bunker owned a house in New York City, hired a housekeeper and helped his son in-law through university. Most had Sundays off: no shopping, no public transit, no movies or restaurants, no trucks on the highway. Business was closed by the Lord's Day Act, a legal tradition in Christian nations since the 17th century. God requires a day of rest, even for slaves and workhorses (Exodus 23:12). These laws were struck down as unconstitutional, because they only served Christians. That's right—sort of—but the constitutionally valid solution was to eliminate a day off for all, rather than require one chosen by each. Again, legislation sounds progressive but guarantees profit. By 2005, both parents were working 40 hours a week or more, on any day of the year, to pay for the same "middle-class" lifestyle, although more of it was made of disposable plastic, and older parents were averaging half as many children. What had required 40 hours/week of work in 1965 required 80 hours+ of work in 2005, with fewer children and longer commutes. In many cases we are comparing the same houses, some of which have lasted over a century already, to newer houses made of cheaper materials with shorter expected lifespans.

Tuition provides another example of the falling value of wages: tuition for my first 2 years at U of T was under $1000 a year. At that time, 1986, minimum wage was $5/hr. There were 10 weeks of summer holidays after high school (16 weeks for university students), so if you worked full-time, you could gross $2000. It was reasonable for you to pay your own tuition, even if you had to borrow for other expenses ($7800 after 4 years, for me). By 2010, tuition had risen to $8000 but minimum wage was still under $10: it sounds like wages doubled, but the most you could earn was half your tuition instead of double it. Living expenses grew in proportion. This increases the debt load of students trying to access those better paying jobs, which they will have to pay back with interest from less-valuable wages.

Older wage slaves contrive many examples of falling wages, remembering things like how long we worked in our youth for our first car, a pack of cigarettes, a gallon of gas, or a case of beer.

And then we ask...

Where the fuck did all the money go?

Where are all the benefits of social cooperation, the division of labour and scale, augmented by technology? Life should be easier. In fact social scientists in the 1970s talked about the "leisure society" we would become as machines and computers took over and we'd work 20 hours a week. Yet, our lives became more difficult in spite of our cooperation, scale, and new technology. Labour hours were doubled, not cut in half.

The value created by doubling the labour required to buy the same lifestyle has not disappeared. It moved to another's ledger, and is the Wealth Gap often cited: Business Owners getting richer, and fewer, and wage-slaves getting poorer, and more numerous. And more plasticky. When you spend your money on clothes and get plastic fibres instead of wool or hemp, you are getting fewer labour-hours back for your money, in the form of a low-quality product that looks like a real one, and water polluted with plastic fibres. Just like when you buy a house that is stick-framed with vinyl siding and shingles, instead of the 3 layers of brick and a metal roof that is a still-standing Victorian home. Requiring more labour to buy the same home or product means that the value of wages fell in one way, while swapping out that product with one that needs replacement sooner reduced the value of wages in another. The first means you have to work longer, and the second means you get less for your money. Both create profit for Business.

The falling value of wages, or deflation, is the aggregate effect of increased profit-taking from a wage-slave perspective, represented by the Wealth Gap. Business makes a circular argument, by calling deflation "inflation" and blaming it on rising prices they cannot control, rather than on falling wages. Perspective. Business sees capital growing where wage slaves see their social power diminishing. *Capital* is money not needed for consumption, available for investment, and in this form remains a class commodity, because one has the social power of an Owner to the extent that they have *extra* cash, after their expenses are paid. When you exercise that power by spending on consumption as planned, it's gone.

From a Business perspective, the falling value of money is the reason to invest cash rather than hide it in a mattress. While Business profits from the labour of wage slaves, it acquires those profits in the same deflating currency when wages come back as sales or taxes. The capital attached to those profits is similarly unstable. It was not always so. Understanding why Business Owners left the Gold Standard for the money used to pay wages helps us see that wage deflation is what Government calls "managing the economy".

Originally, wage slaves were paid with the same money that Business Owners used. This money was based on the Gold Standard, which means notes could be exchanged for a fixed amount of gold at any time. Its value was not subject to deflation any more than the value of gold. However, wage slaves' right to save their gold, rather than spend it, is cited as one of the causes of the Great Depression, some 50 years after the Civil War settled wage slavery as the norm. Their saved capital was a reserve of social power. People could wait, spend it when they were too old to work, or decide themselves about investing it. But the chimera said that wage slaves were supposed to circulate their money back to Business Owners, not secure their own future. Not circulating it back, coming to the bank vaults to retrieve their own gold instead, undermined the Business Owners' economy.

This economic crisis was reminiscent of the spectre of paying wages to plantation slaves, and suggests that the South was correct in predicting that it would undermine their Owners' social power over time. What would Business Owners do if wage slaves were free? They might have to grow their own food, build their own house, do their own work. Absurd. The chimera taught me not to go there.

To prevent wage slaves from being able save capital, Business detached wages from capital, to a great extent, by separating money from gold.

Between 1929 and 1933 in Canada, the US and Europe, wage slaves were ordered by Government to turn in their gold and gold notes because their personal pension plans caused the Business Owners' Great Depression. This was part of the New Deal reform package that established control over interest rates and the paper-money supply, provided the first farm subsidies, and *mandatory pension programs* ("social security"). In exchange for their gold coins, bullion or gold notes, wage slaves received what is called "fiat money", printed by the Government with no guaranteed exchange value. *Fiat* means "a formal authorization or decree". This ability for Government to print money and change its value at will is described as "flexibility" from a Business perspective. Government says flexibility is necessary to keep money circulating and their economy growing.

Gold again became a class commodity—Business didn't stop representing capital with gold, but it stopped paying wage slaves with it. Fiat money provided a flexible currency for wage slaves to trade with; being able to deflate the value of wages meant slaves could save wages without limiting the power of capital, as when wages were paid in capital. Wage slaves would be pressured by currency deflation to either spend it or invest it rather than save it, which means it circulates back to the Business Owners' economy, as planned. Mandatory pension contributions would make it seem as though this was all done on our behalf, but they make it that much harder to save something we could decide what to do with.

Coming back to where we started this history of currency, the fact that Business realizes profits in the same deflatable fiat money now used to pay wages means that their cash reserves lose value at the same rate as our wages. This is the reason to invest money, urgently, in more stable forms of capital, like stocks, bonds, real estate and gold, maybe a new venture or expansion, rather than hide it in a mattress like we used to do with gold.

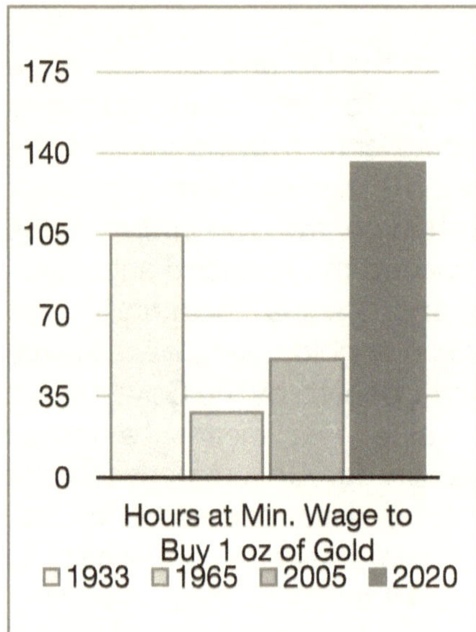

When money and gold were parted, gold was worth $26.33 an ounce, or 105 hours at a minimum wage of 25 cents/hour. Gold cost $35 an ounce in 1965, or 28 hours at a minimum wage of $1.25, reflecting significant improvements in wage slaves' standard of living; but gold was worth $513 in 2005, or about double at 51 hours at a minimum wage of $10. The spot price of gold as I write in January 2020 is over $1500, or 136 hours at an average minimum wage of $11.02. The value of gold, or capital, increases inversely in proportion to the falling value of wages. This reflects the accumulation of value from wage slaves over time, the Wealth Gap. We could say the same about many other forms of capital, such as stocks or real estate.

From a wage slave perspective, the value of wages fell significantly since 1965. From a Business Owner perspective, the value of capital, their investments and the stock market—all increased, growing the Wealth Gap. The rationality of pursuing a job as a means to fulfilling your needs declined in proportion with the value of wages. Young workers expecting their efforts to bring rewards in proportion as they had for their parents are living under an illusion, like we were. A chimera's trick.

These social shell games were designed to maintain the circulation of capital while limiting wage slaves' ability to acquire

34

it. This might suggest that Business Owners were possessed by a different demon than the middle-class chimera. But the chimera has many faces, and all are managed between carrot and stick. To blame the Owners alone is like being one of millions of rats running on a giant wheel picking up speed, and blaming the damage it does on a few spokes for making it roll. The work-spend-work wheel rolls as fast as the rats run. Most of the time, when wage slaves find themselves with a little capital, they consume it on the accoutrements of the Business Class, like fine dinners, clothes, motor vehicles, or travel, and so remain in their class, as planned. When a wage slave succeeds, they are pressured to roll with their new social role, to behave as other Business Owners in running their Business. Rats. They may not want to, may struggle with these choices, but the threat of failing and becoming a wage slave again themselves is real. The social pressure to play the Business Owner's role, or a Politician's role, is no different than the fear of being jobless and homeless that drives oil-pipeline workers to defend oil, debt encumbered cash croppers to defend their chemicals, or the role we play when we stop and buy coffee and doughnuts despite the politics—the people—involved in the global trade of coffee, sugar, and grain.

Most feel as though they have no choice, and end up using others in turn as they are used themselves. Most are at least dimly aware that corruption pervades because they see it where they work, and where they look the other way rather than risk getting fired for talking about it. Plantation slavery, low quality-food, children mining rare earths for cell phones, oil wars in Nigeria, banana republics, dumping the wrong drugs or some chemicals into our intestines or dumping a lot of plastic into the ocean.... these are the things that make our economy roll.

Therefore, these vicious features describe the capitalist, consumerist economy as a whole, not the Business Owners or the wage slaves as people, with fear and anxiety at their root.

At 8 hours a day and with 8 hours sleep, our work life comprises 50%+ of our waking life and, therefore, determines the character of the majority of our social relationships as economic relationships. Competition for jobs, like competition between businesses, or bickering for the best price, makes our social relationships antagonistic, competitive, stressful. People talk as though the anxiety and depression experienced by our youth is a medical problem, rather than anxiety and depression being a rational, human reaction to this social condition. As I write, President Trump, speaking for the US Government, is saying "our economy is the best it's ever been."

From the planet's perspective, it makes no difference what kind of rat you are on the wheel, the damage is the same. Market Capitalism turns our worst characteristics into virtues.

The middle-class chimera is a demon. See it? Fear it.

1.5 Economic Crisis

From the perspective of a wage slave, the social power of capital to create profit depends on economic growth. Human and environmental degradation are consequences of exercising this power, since these resources have no value to Business except as they may be used for profit. Another consequence is the falling value of wages, or deflation of the money used to pay wage slaves, which enables the movement of wealth from wage slaves to Business Owners. The resulting Wealth Gap reflects the reality of wage slaves having to work longer to get less over time. Constant competition for carrots and fear of sticks drives us to do bad things and suffer consequences to our mental and physical health, and this is when the economy is running smoothly.

History shows market capitalism is also subject to periodic crises. Like the Civil War and Great Depression, these are events where the social conditions which allow the market to function are threatened. More recent examples include but are not limited to: the Labour Crisis (1970's); the credit crisis

(1980's); the FarmAid crisis (1985-ongoing); and the sub-prime mortgage crisis (2007–10). The Covid-19 crisis just started. During these crises, whatever intervention is done to repair the "free market" merely sets us up for the next crisis, suggesting that those who exercise control over the economy are nevertheless not in control of it.

For example, exercising control over interest rates and the money supply solved Business' growing pains in the Depression. Managing the intermediate farm crises with subsidies (which were needed right away) and mortgage crises with bail outs; funding foreign development to increase trade; and undertaking military campaigns to prevent trade partners from being socialists, have resulted in huge Government debt. If they increase interest rates in order to restrain debt, they will not be able to manage their own debt. How will they solve the next crisis? This tool is ineffective now: raise rates and both Government and consumers go bankrupt, lowering them is just about impossible. Perhaps Business will buy the debt and privatize all services. Many suffer during these crises, as if all social cooperation had been suddenly swept away, and they are in poverty, even though little in the world changed from one day to the next.

Currently many believe the next crisis will be concerned with debt. I want to draw attention to a larger pattern here: economic crises transfer value rapidly to Business Owners. While Business Owners discuss these crises as if something is very wrong, remember how this judgment is tied to GDP in ways that do not reflect the quality of people's lives. The resolution of a crisis is a bigger Wealth Gap: fewer Business Owners with more wealth, and more wage slaves with less. While the value of wages temporarily increases during a recession, and this is good for wage slaves, from a Big Business perspective, this opportunity to shut down or acquire competition is also good, not bad. They end up with a bigger share of the market when growth starts again, which is more capital. Repeated crises were key historically in creating our situation, where we talk about The 1%, or the 8 men who own 1/2 the world's capital, but keep circulating our time and money towards them through the Business cycle.

Consumer debt is at record highs, in relation to assets. Where did the credit come from? Record-low interest rates were part of the solution to the sub-prime mortgage crisis, along with bail-outs for major banks, GM and Chrysler. Low rates made money cheaper for Government bail outs, and cheaper to borrow for Business and consumers alike. In case you're not aware, banks do not have the money they lend; they are required only to have 5% of these assets. The rest is created by declaring a number on the debt side of the ledger, and the money comes into existence when you pay it back, plus interest, with money you earned. It's good to be a bank.

Wage slaves did borrow. Individually, the amount that they qualify to borrow is measured in relation to their assets and ability to make monthly payments. For wage slaves in North America, that asset is usually a house, partly owned and partly mortgaged, and the payments come from wages. The housing market had been rising in populated cities, which meant investors could make huge profits buying a house and selling a year or two later.

So, let's say you lived in a $100 000 house which was 1/2 asset, 1/2 mortgage; a year or two later, your house is evaluated at $200 000. Now it looks like you have $150 000 in asset and still $50 000 mortgage: it looks like you own 3/4 of your house instead of 1/2. This is called "asset inflation" in Business language, and makes one's balance sheet, their debt-to-asset ratio, look better on paper for the purpose of determining further credit-worthiness. Maybe you'll borrow that $150 000 now and get a boat, a motorcycle, a bigger house, or just eat up credit a bit at a time, leveraged against the asset in your house.

It's a chimera's trick. Asset inflation makes a windfall appear that really exists for Business Owners, but is a shell game for home-owning wage slaves. In the same way that capital is *extra* cash, not needed for consumption, asset inflation in housing only leads to free capital if it is an *extra* house, not needed to live in.

The problem is that while the market value of your home increased, your capital, the social power you command, is still just $50 000, because you now own 1/4 of a home instead of 1/2, *relative to the similarly inflated value of all the other houses in your market.* The new market value of your home is based on the actual sale price of 2% to 3% of homes in your market, so those few sales justified adding $100 000 asset to every homeowner's balance sheet. Owners who bought it as an investment and do not have to live in it realize the *extra* $100k in market value as capital, free cash now, by selling the *extra* house. Some people retire and exit the city in these circumstances (or go Deliberate), like selling stocks at their peak and exiting the stock market. But if you sell and like most have to buy a house to live in, in the same market, the new house also inflated, leaving no extra cash. If you are new to this market it is harder to buy houses.

Your debt-to-asset ratio changed on your balance sheet but the social pressure to keep your job in reality has increased. You would see this reflected in the fact that your mortgage is the same: at Time 1, you had a $100k house, a $50k asset and a $50k mortgage. At Time 2, you sell the house inflated to $200k and buy another house inflated to $200k with the same money, and still have a $50k mortgage. Although you feel like you gained something, your mortgage payments or the number of labour hours needed to pay it did not change. The portion of your wages that used to buy 1/2 of *your* house now buys 1/4, *whether you moved or not.* All are farther from being free from the necessity of a job than before.

Asset inflation has meant that all wage slaves lost wage value, while the mystique created on homeowners' balance sheets made them credit-worthy for more dollars to spend somewhere else. This created an avenue through which Business may part wage slaves from the capital in their real estate, rather than a windfall. Just as separating wages from gold with flexible currency distanced wages from capital, the flexible currency used to assess the market value of housing results in a flexible asset and a flexible debt, paid from flexible wages. A shell game.

Most people buy a more expensive home, rather than one of equal value, fulfilling images of middle-class prosperity or needing space for children. The dollar-number attached to your house has risen, but it still houses the same number of people, and the inflated dollar-number attached to it is similarly attached to the next one. Unfortunately, the bank said "you're richer than you think", and many took advantage of the credit offered based on asset inflation and now carry debt equal to the asset value of their house. So they don't own anything anymore, and are stuck where they live, working and making payments.

The Debt Crisis comes—as it did already with the sub-prime mortgage scandal, and as it does on an individual scale all the time—when something happens to de-stabilize the inflated market value of those homes, which are the assets against which debt is leveraged. If the local economy goes bust, you lose your job, interest rates rise, or climate change puts you in an uninsurable flood or fire zone, and your $200k house deflates to $100k again, then you owe more for your assets than they are worth (which is technical insolvency). It will only make sense to declare bankruptcy, give your house to the bank, and start over with nothing. Some people wait until they can't juggle payments anymore (which is actual insolvency). Repeat a million times: that's our next economic crisis. The outcome of playing this shell game is that your home disappears from your balance sheet, maybe you rent it.

1.6 Wage Slavery versus Deliberate Production

So far, we have seen how the basic structure of market capitalism is designed to recover a wage slave's wages, which from the wage slave's perspective means that economic progress is unlikely. It also establishes our economic relationships—the people we work with and buy commodities from—as antagonistic relationships, sources of anxiety and depression, rather than sources of community or cooperation. Deliberate Economics shows a viable alternative to the work-spend-work wheel.

Getting control of this situation requires not behaving like a wage slave anymore. Slay the chimera, rather than serve it. If you found yourself in a boxing ring, you'd defend yourself by raising your fists, like a boxer. When you find yourself a wage slave, defend yourself by focusing on self-interest and profit, tracked with accurate accounting, like an Owner-Operator. Fundamentally, it is a battle of ideas.

Let's say that every week, you buy a case of beer, or some other treat, for $20. No judgement is intended about your tastes (I'm having a beer now). You might reason that, if you earn $20 an hour at work, this treat costs just one hour and is therefore cheap, even though you'll save only a different $20 from your pay through mandatory pension contributions. Most workers spend their last dollar somewhere.

However, this is bad accounting. As a business, if you were calculating profit for the week in question, you'd take out both the deductions that come off of your pay, and your operating costs for the week. Operating costs include rent/mortgage, car payments, food, clothes,.... I wasn't being generous in not judging your treat, because when you're tracking profitability in dollars like a Business, it doesn't matter whether money was spent on heroin and high-heels or life-saving surgery: it is spent. Money recognizes no other kind of value than other money:

"Profit" in Business accounting is the money left from revenue (money) after expenses (money).

Whether you save the $20 somewhere else and buy the beer the bottom line is the same.

Like any Owner-Operator, you have a limited number of billable hours (or work hours), but your operating costs are 24/7. Extra cash now is a stronger kind of capital than a mandatory pension contribution or mortgage principle because you can choose how to use it. A pension plan can fail, or you could die first; and you may not be able to get ahead by selling your house. Either way, if all you could save from a 40-hour week is $20, then $20 is your profit for the week, and you worked for 50 cents an hour, not the $20 your employer spent. The rest was operating costs, needed just to keep working. If you made that treat yourself, or didn't buy it, then your profit would double.

How much would your wages be worth if you started on a Deliberate path, and began producing some of your food, housing or heat Deliberately?

A quick example: let's say organic carrots sell for $2/pound. That sounds so cheap it's not worth doing, and suburbanites invest their capital in lawns instead. $2 sounds like 6 minutes at $20 an hour, but that's the bad accounting again. 6 minutes of my time really is a good estimate of the labour required to produce a pound of carrots, once a garden is established (capital). Most carrots (those for late fall and winter use) are planted right after garlic harvest in July, since digging the garlic means I just loosened and weeded more-than-enough soil. A few minutes to smooth it with a rake and plant. Whether you want 10 pounds or 50, much of your time is getting the seeds and rake together and put away after. Weed and thin once, an hour for the whole bed, pick them. But the worker above trades 4 hours at 50 cents an hour to buy carrots, just once, not the 6 minutes required to produce them. It might take 6 minutes to buy them.

Wage slavery seems really hard because it is—we're only talking about carrots! Economically, these carrots represent any marginal improvement in lifestyle: maybe it is medicine you need, maybe it is the start of saving social power. And even if you buy the carrots, they're these little sticks that a machine could pick. Often, for me, a pound of carrots is one carrot.

While we are in the carrot bed, note that fresh greens in the next bed lose 90% of their vitamin C within 24 hours of being picked. The plant needs to feed off itself, trying to stay alive, heal the wound where it was cut, rather than succumb to bacteria and fungi, and rot, which it will in time. So you can't actually buy fresh greens, if *fresh* means "nutritionally optimal" rather than "won't make you sick". The only way to get them is to pick them right before you eat them. Salad greens from the grocery store are literally a decaying replica of what a salad should be. Produce that has travelled the world, well...

Once we start comparing the accounting of wage slavery with Deliberate production, we start paying attention to labour time, the quality of that time, and the quality/quantity of the outcome, as common points of comparison between these economies. Like debating plantation versus wage slavery, evaluating which is the more efficient mode of production, and which is the more humane, means that we must compare what we get for what we do, outputs over inputs. If a Deliberate approach gets me better carrots in 6 minutes than those I can trade for 4 hours of wage slavery, then the Deliberate approach is a more efficient way to get carrots. When we hear about Business Executives earning an average years' wages in under a week, we can see how, from their perspective, it may be more efficient to buy old carrots.

But from the perspective of a wage slave, reflecting upon the Social Pie argument as a guideline, investing my wages in a carrot market is a waste of my time. time is the only money i got.

Wage slavery and Deliberate production are fundamentally different economies, with different goals, and can be represented by different equations:

Business Accounting: **Revenue - Expenses = Profit**
In a wage slave perspective: **Money - Money = Money**

Deliberate Accounting: **Labour Time + Resources = Use Value**

In the Business Owners' economy, wage slaves—you—are an expense whose price is tied to production cost, and the point of your labour is to create profit for your employer. If you're doing well, that's the signal to deflate your wages. In a Deliberate Economy, you are not a commodity or expense utilized in the profit chain. Instead, you are the reason why commodities are required and your labour is engaged. If you are doing well, you succeeded. Production is evaluated in terms of fulfilling your needs, or use value, rather than market value.

Use value is a different currency than fiat money, or market value.

Use value is all that matters to Deliberate Economics. With carrots, that is the nutrition and flavour that come out, contributions to health and sustenance. With firewood, it is heat. They keep you alive but in different ways. Most find satisfaction from autonomy, and prefer working without a boss.

Market value only matters for the purpose of buying and selling (trade) and is independent of use value. $20 worth of heroin and high heels, $20 of life saving surgery, $20 towards a pension, $20 for beer, $20 income tax, all have the same value: $20.

Use value is a broader concept— it is a *flexible* currency— because it captures the value differences between commodities like heroin and high heels, or life saving surgery, or free time, or even money, as the different kinds of profit they are. It does not require you to express all of those values as a money value and crunch them into the same equation, like GDP. Because there is no place in Business accounting to track any kind of value besides market value, it is easy to lose track of losses like nutrition levels, health or environmental problems, or anxiety and stress. Business cannot acknowledge improvements in these use values as profit, because they aren't money. Market values and use values are *incommensurable*, which means that you can never express one in terms of another, or all in terms of money, without losing what made it valuable in the first place. Hence, the market takes no notice when those values leave our lives.

Labour time required to obtain use values of all kinds is a quantifiable common point of comparison. Anyone can calculate the number of labour hours required to acquire use value regardless of their national currency, to arrive at specific numbers about the falling value of their own wages.

Resources have an inestimable value and each their own, where some are gone forever when we use them, and some come back in time. It follows from the Deliberate Accounting equation that less is better, regardless of how we represent that value in a particular calculation.

Deliberate Production has many advantages:

Deliberate production is protected from wage/currency deflation by not relying on money. It never takes longer to produce a carrot or hammer a nail than before, so the use value of your labour is constant when applied Deliberately rather than traded for deflatable wages. Once debt-free, you are protected from asset inflation as well, which makes the value of labour time used to make your assets as stable as the value of gold.

Deliberate production is protected from the vagaries of the market by not participating in it. Recently, for example, bad weather on one side of the country caused $8 cauliflower on the other, and positive press for the benefits of celery more than doubled celery to $7 when it was in season. Conflict between Politicians meant pork and canola prices fell at the expense of farmers in North America, while their usual market in China went without. While the market value of a commodity responds to events anywhere in the system, Deliberate production has only local weather to worry about, so is protected from these vagaries. Generally, bad weather for one crop is good for another, so if one does fail, that just means you'll eat more of something else this year. Hail decimated my garden one year in the last 30. This meant I bought one bag of potatoes and one of onions. While much of the rest may have been damaged and unmarketable, or smaller, it was fine to eat or process for storage, or escaped the hail by being harvested before or planted after the event.

A related difference is the absence of competition between Deliberate producers, beyond bragging rights for the biggest carrot. Market competitors have an antagonistic relationship whether they are wage slaves competing for the same job, or Businesses competing for the same market. Another farmer growing carrots increases supply, and so reduces the market value of everyone's carrots. As a Deliberate producer, your carrots do not reduce the use value of mine, so I bear you no secret ill will for trying. Our relationship to each other is no longer antagonistic. I may even want to help, or we could cooperate, or just give each other what we have too much of— this is not a trade—instead of seeing it spoil. I would rather not have to see you buy it if it costs me nothing to appear generous. Big grocery stores would rather see it spoil, because you wouldn't buy it if they gave it to you. Where market competition implies a zero-sum game in which some players' prosperity requires other players' losses, so helping is a sacrifice, Deliberate Economics recognizes that if I have carrots and you have carrots, then *we* have carrots, and *we* are better off. We have time to celebrate and the food to do it with. It's in my interest to help. No Sacrifice.

The fact that profit is realized as use value rather than market value changes what counts as a goal in production. The Business Owner's equation favours products that wear out quickly or need expensive replacement parts because that results in more money at the end. The equation in Deliberate Economics favours products that last forever, because that results in more value. De-Growth follows from the individual pursuit of profit in Deliberate Economics.

From a Business Owner perspective, *our gain is their loss*, measured by the amount that Global GDP De-Grew by removing the buying and selling of carrots from the Business Owners' economy. While Business accounting loses track of use values, our increased use value shows up as series of losses.

From a planet perspective, we have eliminated purchased fertilizers, pesticides, food miles, and packaging (losses to GDP), and compared to AgriBusiness we have utilized a higher portion of our harvest, which means more use value from our labour and resources—more Deliberate profit. It is illegal in Canada to sell forked carrots, and the chimera doesn't accept misshapen produce anyway, but everybody who gardens gets some and eats them, rather than throw them out, as must market-value farmers with too many forked carrots to eat by themselves.

A comparison between wage slave and Deliberate production of carrots therefore shows that wage slavery wastes much of our labour and resources because *the efficiency generated by Business is an efficiency in using money to create more money, not efficiency in using human and natural resources to create use value.*

1.7 Deliberate Economics and Opportunity Cost: The Experiment

Market capitalism makes economic progress difficult for wage slaves by deflating the value of wages, creating social and environmental problems as a consequence of growth. The point is to reveal how a Deliberate life creates a path to freedom from this oppression, and results in De-Growth. Get more by doing less. Producing something Deliberately means that the object of your labour is the object of your intention, so you get food by growing it, housing by building it, heat by gathering firewood, and so on. Most people imagine this is more difficult than their job, and so it sounds like they are being asked to make a sacrifice.

My experience with both approaches taught me that a Deliberate approach is more efficient, and more humane, than trying to meet these needs as a wage slave. No sacrifice.

Around February 1995, I set aside my Doctoral thesis to live Deliberately, as an experiment. A successful defence depended on Deliberate Economics being true, and the chimera would be in the room to challenge it. My examiners were the best in my area. I was qualifying to be one of them. My thesis was that a job—like *our* job—was unprofitable from an economic perspective—and *we* were contributing to wage deflation and environmental problems just by participating in the economy, regardless of how sincerely *we* debated and wrote. Because we were recirculating money, running on the wheel. I was breaking ranks with our own principles: a capitalist critique of capitalism. Groucho Marx once joked that he wouldn't belong to a club that would have him as a member, but this was no joke. Just as the chimera drives pipeline workers to defend oil, *employed* Philosophers defend their role in society right where they are. Showing up at the defence better off economically than others at the same stage of our careers would prevent arguing that it can't work, silence the chimera. The defence went better than most, done in a couple of hours, but the social awkwardness was palpable throughout.

It never went away. However, I have longer experiments to demonstrate Deliberate Economics with 20 years later, including trying wage slavery myself for 12 years:

I started a Community Shared Agriculture project, called the Oasis Project, on a small plot borrowed from friends in California, Ontario, and delivered shares of a big garden weekly to 10 shareholders who put up cash. Shareholder farming was mostly unheard of. The next year I borrowed for vacant land up the road in Keelerville and expanded to a 2-acre garden, corrected some errors, delivered weekly to 40 shareholders and sold high-end produce to restaurants.

Growing a wide variety of crops meant that this apparent market activity provided me with a similar variety to eat, whether or not anything sold. It also meant that I was already on land, so could efficiently use free time, even in small amounts, to work on other needs. Picking up stones for a few minutes a day resulted in a level lawn, and an attractive wall to act as a safety barrier at the edge of a cliff.

In year 4, I borrowed for materials and built an off-grid house. A parameter of the Oasis Project was complying with all laws. The local building code required me to build the house 960 square feet rather than start with 600 and add to it *if needed;* this law exists to undermine using fair market value to determine property taxes by setting a bottom to those values. More house is good for Business because it will generate more property tax and consume more material and maintenance until it falls apart. I had already built a 100 square-foot greenhouse and attached a 100 square-foot cabin to live in during the first 4 springs, all from recycled windows and wood. Candles and oil lamps for the first 5 years, and then built a small solar and wind system, and got a fridge to replace the ice box.

By year 5 I had stopped farming for income and completed the PhD, but continued to live Deliberately for a total of 12 years on that property. Part-time renovation work was more efficient than selling vegetables for cash requirements, and gave me more freedom to organize my time. Sounds rustic I know, and I pretty much had winters off. I need to say that again, "winters off", so that no one confuses the time requirements with those of a full-time job, even though I worked hard at the start, given my decision to go all-in for this experiment. No regrets. Most careers start out rough.

To round out my story, I took a teaching job for 12 years and sold the Oasis Project, then quit that job to live Deliberately again. Tried it both ways. Let's look at the accounting.

"Opportunity cost" estimates the results of what you could have done with your labour (or your money) and compares it with alternatives, or with what actually happened. Investing time in one activity means that you lost the opportunity to invest that time in another. If you go to one place you spent the opportunity to be in another at the same time. If you eat too much dinner there is no room for dessert. Choices bear opportunity costs.

For this comparison, let's say that instead of the Oasis Project, I completed the PhD on time and then taught at the University of Toronto. It would have been unrealistic to expect that position, even if it existed, being fresh out of graduate school. My real-life choices were starting positions, the rough start of a career, so my actual opportunities were worse economically, which is the point. This was the job I trained for, my middle-class chimera to slay.

The starting salary for full-time Professors was about $50 000 a year, and I would have to live in Toronto. That would mean no opportunity to grow food or cut firewood, no place to build a house, and not enough pay to buy one. I'd need new clothes, and have to eat whatever I could buy in the city, breathe that air. Friends who lived in Toronto at the time thought I would have no savings, even with what sounded like a prestigious middle-class job. If I could save $5000 a year, the 10% of gross recommended by Business as a profit margin, that would be ideal, but few manage to do it. It would have amounted to $60 000 after 12 years, if I had managed to save it. Most likely, these assets would be realized as mandatory pension contributions, and so inaccessible at the start of my career, when I needed my earnings to get out from under rent or mortgage interest so I could save for retirement, rather than being forced to save for retirement before securing a place to live.

By contrast, I garnered $12 000 to15 000+ a year in money as a subsistence farmer, selling some produce and doing renovation work in the nearby town. Doesn't sound like much, but, with a mortgage payment of $152/month ($27,000 for building material), low food and utility costs, I was able to save $6000 to $9000 of it, or pay down the mortgage, or add an asset like solar power, all of which are on the asset-side of the balance sheet. $6000 saved from $12 000 in revenue is a 50% profit margin, and more money absolutely than 10% of $50 000, by $1000, in the worst year. Remember the Social Pie argument? 50% of a small pie I baked was more pie than my share of the big one society baked, in fact rather than theory. Participating in food and housing markets, making them bigger, did not make me better off than making my own.

Did I mention winters off—time to do things like finish a PhD or bake pies? This wasn't a full-time job. Manuals on self sufficiency agree that it takes about 4 hours a day to look after your food, heat and housing, once you're set up. Often the word "work" is associated only with wage slave agreements, as the time we spend "at work". In this sense, the line between "work time" and "your time" gets blurred because it includes canning your tomatoes or watering your garden, but in the absence of a boss. Having several months of food and fuel in storage before planting time and a place to live is Deliberate capital. It gives you the social power to choose how you spend your time (profit), and how you seek more money, if you need it. We cannot attach a price to organic food all the time, real meals, no commute, the quality difference in one's day-to-day life. It is a mistake to think these numbers are small because they were generated 20 years ago: they were small numbers at the time but commanded significant social power when others were working for 50 cents an hour.

I lived there for 12 years, having put a total of $87 000 towards the land and materials over that time, and sold the works for

$130 000. By then the mortgage had been paid, so this was all asset I didn't have before. Unlike a pension, I had access to it right away.

Comparing the Oasis Project ($130 000 now) with its best-case opportunity cost ($60 000 towards a pension at retirement) demonstrates that I was better off as a subsistence farmer with a renovation sideline than as a University Professor. Economically more efficient.

The "experiment" was about whether a Deliberate life was also more humane.

Building houses or farming for wages are good jobs for carpenters and farmers, but the chimera said building a house and growing food for myself, the same labour, was beneath *me*, a waste of my fine talents, absurd. A PhD who ends up labouring is a failure. What does that say about the carpenter and farmer, whose labour this Professor feels a right to? Sorting these ideas was my personal battle with the middle-class chimera, reflected in the social awkwardness of talking about economics with anyone in the middle class.

> *"He was but seven and twenty, an age... at which they are hopeful of achievement, resolute in avoidance, thinking that Mammon shall never put a bit in their mouths and get astride their backs, but rather that Mammon, if they have anything to do with him, shall draw their chariot."*
>
> *—George Eliot, Middlemarch, 1872*

The value of starting in humble circumstances is clarity about what happiness requires. When we strip life to essentials and go camping or travel to another culture, we later remember those occasions as some of life's finest: this unburdening is part of the motive behind vacations, and in this sense a Deliberate life becomes all vacation. Our slavery is vacated forever. I learned that once my animal nature is satisfied, or once I am well fed, sheltered, and a little tired, nothing brings more joy than company. Any*thing* after that was a kind of *extra*. Shiny things or titles like Professor may have brought a brief distraction, but since in reality these things did not make me better off, neither did I experience their absence as any kind of loss: the only thing I was "going without" was extra burden. My personal battle with the chimera required understanding that my slavery was a choice made by *a vague image of myself and that which I aspired to become*. Do I work and spend to live, or to satisfy some image of social status that makes me better than you? Resisting social power made it clear that the price of conformity to these images had been my humanity, and I could choose. Those first nights in my cabin, I fell asleep unable to shake the image of myself leaping though a paper barrier.

A key lies in seeing money as one commodity among others, rather than seeing all in terms of money. Some commodities, like tools and property taxes, can only be obtained with money. While the market values of commodities are changing all the time, the use-values of commodities like food and housing and the labour to produce them are stable and predicable. Spend Deliberately, because spending money means buying labour and commanding social power, which empowers someone else in the economy. Use cash when possible, everybody saves. Business Owners advise that credit is for things that make money, but the lion's share of how they use their own money takes this one step further: money is only for things that make money—hence, avoid consuming it. Avoid shell games.

A great source of profit was building my house with my own labour. If one pays 1/3 of their wages to a mortgage for 30 years, it takes 10 years' labour to acquire a home, perhaps 1/3 of 2 peoples' wages today, or 20 years' labour. That is more work than squaring logs with axes as pioneers had done, or stacking rocks and mud as many in the world still do. The point of this comparison is that you'd get a house faster and easier than 20 years' labour, even if you stacked or packed until walls were 4 feet thick, and so shows that years of labour are lost by obtaining housing through wage slavery.

In my case it took from June to December, with the help of a few friends and along with the market garden, to get an insulated shell up and drywalled to move into, and a few months of finishing afterwards. One year, along with farm activities, not 10 or 20. The land had been paid for by then ($27 000 + 3 years' shares in the garden for the seller), leaving a small mortgage for materials ($152/month). I had estimated an asset increase of $30 000 that year, by following the contractor's practice of using the cost of materials to estimate the cost of labour. If I had received $30 000 as wage income that year, as the contractor paid to build the house to that point of completion, that $30 000 would have been taxed as income on top of the $12 000 from farming, or as $42 000. I'd have had to earn $51 000 in Canada to net $42 000 after income taxes, more still if we estimated what I would need to earn to save $30 000 after paying for food and housing as a Professor in a city. Therefore, the $50 000 gross salary offered by the Professor job lost the opportunity-cost comparison with a Deliberate approach, and there was no magic or luck involved in coming out twice as far ahead, just good business based on accurate accounting.

From a tax perspective, the full market value of the house remains tax sheltered within lifetime capital gains limits, and $12 000 annual cash income was below the personal exemption level. We don't list garden produce that we eat on our tax forms. For the Business economy this produce does not exist, just as labour used to build a house has no place in their accounting. The standard practice for evaluating a home built by the owner, for property-tax purposes, is to add the property value and the materials and labour cost together; therefore, spending $0 on labour kept the property evaluated and taxed below market value for as long as I owned it, legally, while meeting municipal house-size requirements.

I took a regular teaching job for the next 12 years. It started as a part-time contract they contacted me about in a bind. I was looking at it like one of my renovation jobs. The salary, although it came with a 2.5-hour commute each way, meant that I could pay what was left of the mortgage in one year, now that this capital—a house to live in, a root cellar full of food and a garden to grow in—had been established, increasing the value of my wages. I got sucked in, obtained tenure in 3 years and was at the top of the salary scale (about $80K), at which time I sold the Oasis Project to cut an hour from the commute.

In hindsight, this had been an opportunity to quit that job instead of sell, to stay on track with my plan. I had not anticipated the chimera returning. The new situation was more ordinary, a mortgage for a bigger house, full-time work, still 3 hours a day in the car. There was no affordable land closer to the job, and I wasn't going to start buying all my food or heating with electricity after knowing better.

I did no better than my colleagues at saving from my wages. I could not save $30 000 in a year from this $80 000 salary, which was closer to $45 000 after taxes and deductions. This salary was responsible for the new mortgage, commuting, new clothes, new computer and other employment costs. These include regular aggravations, like traffic, or not getting lunch together at dawn, so you either eat whatever crap you can buy conveniently or don't eat at all. Once these employment costs were apportioned to the salary responsible, any profits over those years were attributable to the food that I continued to grow and wood that I cut, as well as renovations and additions, except for tied-up pension contributions and tied-up mortgage principal.

That is, I was only getting ahead with money I could use now, capital, to the extent that I continued to live Deliberately. I began producing eggs to sell at school along with honey purchased in bulk from a local beekeeper, which offset some commuting costs, while supplying eggs and honey of the best quality for domestic use.

I took a year without pay, twice, to work with a dedicated team—led by a former student—as the agronomist on a food security project in Sierra Leone (West Africa). We built a rice mill to connect subsistence farmers with their local market, to offset imports and strengthen the local economy. That's another story, though it is also about Deliberately finding profit in efficiencies that improve lives, and gave me the opportunity to see how much of the world lives.

I then got in early on cannabis stocks—only because Deliberate living meant I had some savings when an opportunity that everyone could recognize came up. It was like being around when alcohol prohibition ended, and able to invest pennies in a brewery or distiller.

Cannabis "entered" the Canadian market in the form of publicly traded Corporations. These Corporations entered the stock market as penny stocks, high-risk ventures, because smoking a joint was a new idea the middle class might not accept. Pension funds, like most investment funds, are not permitted to invest in penny stocks. All of our pension plans and mutual funds therefore missed a certain ride from pennies to dollars a share. Wage slaves with a few thousand dollars were able to take advantage, along with existing cannabis dealers, who moved their free market profits into the Business Owners economy and became legitimate stockholders. A similar opportunity for wage slaves may present itself as cannabis regulation replaces prohibition around the world. My next bet is the electric economy, however, because I see Government policy like the Paris Accord paving the way.

By that time, I had realized I needed a re-exit plan. Wage slavery was a waste of time, and my spirit.

During this pursuit of cash and learning about Business, each year I got more worn-down from the sitting required through the school year, then tried to get back in shape over the summer, but after 10 years I was losing weight and strength. Chimera came back. As scientists are pointing out these days, good health requires moderate exercise every day, not when you have the time. I'm no better than anyone else at exercising for its own sake—this we do Deliberately, when we do it—but regular exercise just happens as a product of Deliberate living. I quit a tenured teaching position and went back to Deliberate living again, having given wage slavery an honest try for about the same amount of time. Back to feeling strong, a healthy weight, and free to do what I want as it snows outside, rather than engage a pre-dawn commute through the city.

Those years were effectively a second life experiment, deploying 12 years of *the same me with the same skills* but as a wage slave. After trying it both ways, they will be the last. The opportunity cost is too high. I admit these numbers also suggest that wage slaves in the top 10%, who make 6 figure salaries, are better off where they are, but only if they do in fact save 10% or more of their gross income after a 40-hour week. The rest of us are forced to accept less.

I moved again, to more and better land with a smaller house in need of some care, and more barn—an even-trade money-wise. A friend moved in and pays some rent—but not enough to create taxable income. He already paid tax, to get the rent money. Any Deliberate life requires some cash, for property taxes and things you don't produce, and whether that is renting a room, selling high-value produce, firewood, hay, pottery, part-time contracts, or stocks, depends on finding the best fit for you and the markets available. Any *other* dollar that comes my way now is savings, capital.

To be clear, if I were to succumb to the chimera, stop producing my food and fuel, or start driving fancy cars or flying on vacations, consumption would create the necessity for a job again, or at least more work. I prefer less work to more, and slew the chimera after a second battle, at 50.

"Retired" is what Business calls a wage slave or a horse when they're no longer useful. I'm not retired, or employed, or unemployed, or a volunteer. I've Deliberately escaped wage slavery, and describe my employment status as "free". That box is not available, if you want auto insurance for example, and my lawyer chose "entrepreneur" as the best option. An Owner-Operator.

1.8. Can I Do This in the City?

I am often asked whether there is an urban version of a Deliberate life. Most people live in cities, which means the process necessarily begins there, like it did for me. Partly this is a question of how to start from different economic and geographic positions. The city is the core of market capitalism, where the consumption of labour and resources are at their peak, and where the chimera makes wage slavery seem ideal. People are drawn to cities either by jobs, or by the ability to spend faster on the accoutrements of Business Owners, or to do both on the work-spend-work wheel. Some believe that they won't be lonely.

Some believe that urban density makes more efficient use of resources. This is true if we compare an urban wage slave to a rural wage slave, because a rural wage slave likely drives further to work, and buys the same commercial, imported, and processed products, from the same global supply chains. A Deliberate life uses labour and resources more efficiently than wage slavery because food miles and packaging are eliminated along with a stressful commute.

We have seen that Business means "efficiency" in using money to make money, rather than efficiency in using labour and resources to create use value. Urban homes cost more than rural homes with the same use value. It would cost a fortune to buy acres of land with a house and barn in a city: more labour is required to obtain similar value. Turning the example around, the rent on a small apartment in Toronto is enough to make mortgage payments on an acreage with a house a few hours' drive away.

Corporate offices are located on the most expensive and congested land. Why would Business find this *more* profitable? If scale, or more people using one service in one place, is more economically efficient, why are taxes higher as urban density increases, not lower?

Follow the road. Driving into a city core means passing Businesses until you get to City Hall, Government.

A city requires all types of roads. The visible pavement can occupy half of its area. Many of these "roads" are solutions to problems introduced by urban density, adding new costs per household that were not there in a rural setting. These solutions add to the environmental footprint of each house at the same time. Stacking houses on top of each other as apartments reduces their environmental footprint only by the area of those houses. The environmental footprint of a human includes the acres of land needed to grow their food, provide their energy, mine their metals, clean their air, manufacture their goods, and eliminate their garbage. It is hard to render this footprint literally as an area of land, but it increases along with the problems of urban density.

Putting a lot of houses into a small area means that each can no longer rely on their own well and septic bed. They can't let rain run off their roof or their roads and soak into the surrounding soil. Basements in tall buildings can go down several stories, which must also be kept dry. Each must contribute to water pipes, toilet sewers and storm sewers. In the city, you must pay to drink, pay to pee, and pay when it rains. Sales of trucked-in-bottled-water prove how many prefer the taste of plastic to their tap water, so water also needs highway space. Electricity and natural gas need their own corridors. All of these roads must be frost-free, open 24/7. They require lighting at night along with buildings, billboards, and intersections. There is little room to grow food or cut wood, or set up a solar array or windmill, so food, energy and other commodities must travel from where they are produced into the city (which produces little) on paved roads or train tracks, or into sea ports, and the garbage must be trucked or piped out. Some of it gets all the way back to China, or ends up in oceans and waterways, buried in the ground, or burnt, and some of it just flies around in the streets. If you talk to your dental hygienist, you may discover that plastic from some brands of toothpaste is stuck in your gums, and if you talk to your doctor, you may discover how much plastic is stuck in your guts.

As urban density increases, Government proposes public transit—more people packed into a smaller space—as the answer to congestion. (?). Perhaps a subway or overhead rail. Note that the argument behind this stacking is the cost of more asset-inflated surface property, which means setting all the buildings back, or removing some, and compared to these concessions, people believe public transit is to their advantage. We are missing the Business perspective if we make the accounting mistake of comparing the cost of driving a car with the cost of riding a subway, when the main cost is the road for either, and when the reason people are creating rush-hour congestion is their job. Business never considers a city full, just ready to grow higher and denser, even if the population will not fit in the streets anymore.

Business Owners benefit most from taxpayer-funded infrastructure. Remember, Government is the bureaucracy that creates the social conditions for profitability. A common cost of Business is the roads that make business profitable. These "roads" include air ports, rail, and seaports. This infrastructure is the real expense of global trade: not the trucks, trains, planes, or ships that goods travel in, but the roads those vehicles travel on, and ports that they travel to. Trucks show up in Business' accounting as their expense but not the infrastructure, or the cost of removing their plastic from our system. Business tells us it must be this way. When we hear about a company considering moving to a city, their first concerns are whether there is adequate infrastructure, an airport, and a trained labour pool. Unless wage slaves pay for infrastructure through their taxes, and so absorb the cost of shipping Business Owners' goods in, taking the garbage out or eating it themselves, and herding trained wage slaves in and out, they won't bring jobs.

That's not the end of it. Recent decades have produced "just-in-time delivery" of retail goods. That means retailers no longer own a warehouse. Instead, they just have a loading dock, regular deliveries on bigger roads, and their merchandise is warehoused in trucks on the highway at the taxpayers' expense. Trucks are cheap, but roads are expensive. The ability to shift warehouse space that business pays for onto highway space that taxpayers build and maintain is precisely why this model improved profitability.

These subsidies challenge the notion that Business is profitable in the ordinary sense of making more money than it spends, and shows that consumers will not pay the full cost of products if the education of workers, the infrastructure (shipping) and the waste-disposal costs were on the price tag instead of hidden in high taxes, our intestines, and pollution yet to be paid for. Under this arrangement, wage slaves don't see it like Business does, or maybe the problem is that they do. Perhaps this is why we have yet to see a Mayoral candidate running on a "Sell City Hall" platform to pay down the city's debt, reduce taxes, reduce downtown congestion, and move services closer to the people who must access them. Having to pay a parking ticket or obtain a parking pass downtown in City Hall, where there is no parking, is just creating aggravation.

In the end, remaining in the city means accepting these extra costs, when avoiding waste, inefficiency, and aggravation are the reasons to pursue a Deliberate path instead. More after-tax income is needed, the pursuit of which results in diminishing returns through progressive rate taxation—get less by doing more. Being close to a smaller city or town may facilitate part time work or a market for domestic products—access to some cash, while avoiding these extra costs: straddling two economies.

However, I may be blinded my own path, not thinking hard enough about other people's starting positions. Just as there are many Businesses, there are many Deliberate paths, and my own began in a city. Any step in this direction is profitable.

Deliberate Economics is adaptable to different circumstances where the economy has failed to support the people. I have Communist Cuba in mind, a different setting economically and geographically. When the USSR dissolved, shipments to Cuba of livestock, feed, fertilizer and pesticides stopped. People were hungry. They started growing food wherever they could: lawns, abandoned parks, boulevards, and balconies or rooftops that could support containers. The absence of commercial inputs meant they produced organically. By 2010, the capital city, Havana, was producing 90% of its food within the city limits. Some groups formed, and began feeding orphans and others in need. Once this part of the food supply was established, when the Cuban Government thought about doing something with those lots, they needed to consult with local agriculture groups.   We could describe these groups as Deliberate Corporations. Even in the city of Havana, ordinary people recovered social power by acting Deliberately.

1.9 Deliberate Revolution & Chicken George Day

Market capitalism uses the social power of capital to control wage slaves, and presents this as a form of social cooperation through which wage slaves are better off than if they tried to meet their needs in a different economic regime, or on their own. Progress on this path is more difficult than a Deliberate approach to meeting the same needs. Part of escaping wage slavery is a battle with the chimera, and means re-evaluating a Good Life as one in which we are thriving personally, while minimizing use of our labour or resources. The most efficient form of economy, and the most humane. Personal financial security, and our common social and environmental goals, are achievable if we apply our efforts more Deliberately.

In Alex Haley's historical novel <u>Roots</u>, Chicken George was the first of Kunta Kinte's descendants to obtain his freedom from plantation slavery in the US. Named for his ability to train fighting chickens for his master's gambling, he began receiving a share of the winnings and was, in time, able to buy his own freedom. My childhood take on the televised version of his story forgot much resistance to agreements to liberate George sooner. Still, his path to freedom, straddling two economies to increase his social power, was unique and ultimately successful. I remembered that part right.

Slavery and feudalism feature prominently in my family history before WW2 in Poland, and during imprisonment in Nazi concentration camps. Perspective. As a child, I sensed something familiar between the whip in my family's history, Chicken George's history, and when my father got up at 4:30 a.m. to drive to the factory. I learned to recognize this familiar element as social power.

Perhaps these histories gave me the idea that a Good Life was embodied in the simple dreams of slaves. Their perspective on what form of economy was the most efficient, and the most humane, was the most clear about the price of humanity, because they paid that price themselves. The one thing clear to a slave is that the most efficient economy, and the most humane, requires no slaves. Ever since, I thought of the day when I would live on my own land without the *necessity* of a job as "Chicken George Day". It turned out that Chicken George Day was not an event, but a process.

Deliberate living is living according to a different model than the chimera has defined for a wage slave. This creates a wedge into market capitalism that is similar to the problem which precipitated the US civil war, liberated Chicken George and liberated me. This wedge is the sword with which to slay the chimera. You're expected to pursue fiat money and consume it all for market commodities, rather than apply your labour Deliberately. Straddling between capitalist and Deliberate economies increases the value of the money that you have or can get, by passing less back to Businesses Owners. Then capital, which is social power, starts to pump back in your direction.

However, Deliberate production will not instigate violence. The Owner-Operator remains a moral ideal: remember, the chimera has many faces. As a capitalist you are expected and encouraged to pursue your self-interest, your profit, because that's good for us. It is a wedge precisely because hardly anyone takes this alternative seriously. Our tax forms remind us of our right to organize our affairs so as to pay the least tax within the law: that's what we are told to do, and what Business does. We must declare the market value of barter exchanges, but we do not assign a market value to food that we produce and eat, or to labour that makes a house to live in, just as we don't attach a market value when we dress ourselves, bathe, or clip our own nails.

Self-interest drives Deliberate Economics, and personal success does not depend on others choosing more Deliberate paths. However, the aggregate effect of people choosing more Deliberate paths is a Deliberate Revolution.

A Deliberate Revolution accomplishes social goals constructively, rather than through violence, protest, petition, or vote. It requires no formal organization or central authority because it is the aggregate effect of individual choices. It does not matter whether 5% quit their jobs, or 50% of us save 10% of our wages by going part of the way. The impact on GDP is roughly 5% De-Growth, and is sufficient to change which Businesses succeed and which fail, shaping the economy while we save. Supposing unemployment to be 5%, if 5% of wage slaves chose to live Deliberately, then unemployment would drop. Remaining wage slaves could negotiate better wages, because they could get a different job for real, not just in principle, thereby alleviating antagonism and insecurity. To the extent that environmental degradation and resource depletion are attributable to bad farming practices, waste in food systems, planned obsolescence, over production, global rather than local production... much of this waste can be eliminated. It's just not profitable for me to invest in those markets.

That's wage slaves exercising their social power. We abandon the most oppressive and unsustainable parts of the market economy in reality. If you don't like AgriBusiness, or slavery, then don't buy their products. If your employment is destructive and unprofitable, then don't do it. When you grow your own food, build your own house, produce your own heat, you not only liberate yourself from having to make money to buy these things, you also liberate the person forced to do it for you. It frees both a producer and a consumer from the equation, which is better for us all, in proportion as it reduces GDP.

De-growth, as a result of individuals finding profit in more efficient production.

Finding profit and efficiencies is what we are supposed to do in a capitalist society. De-Growth follows from accepted capitalist principles when those principles are applied by wage slaves acting like Owner-Operators. We are supposed to withdraw support from Businesses that provide us no profit, because acting against our own self-interest undermines any social benefits a free market could provide. We begin to manage more resources ourselves as Owner-Operators who gain use value from their sustainability.

Since social power under market capitalism is distributed through the circulation of money, not votes, we are a *Moneytalkscracy*, not a Democracy. During elections, we debate issues that have little economic impact but get us angry at each other, in order to elect Business to sign the next trade deal or deflate our wages, but we don't get a say on details of trade deals or the money supply. Votes in the ballot box change little. In a Moneytalkscracy, the jobs that we accept and our purchasing dollars, the same production and consumption that are the circulation of money, are the votes that shape our social world and environment. This is where our social power lies.

The current aggregate consequence of these votes is environmental degradation, a dubious food supply, and workers competing their way to a lower standard of living. These aggregate effects may not have been intended, and all are compelled by the chimera to roll along. By the same reasoning, people Deliberately satisfying exactly the same self-interest, because the economy has failed them, will have a positive aggregate effect on society, the economy, and the environment as a whole. Like it did in Havana.

Business may create barriers to a Deliberate Revolution, or a significant portion of wage slaves becoming free. My freedom exists in an unexploited conceptual space, using the Owner-operator position to manage my capital for use value rather than market value. Like wage slaves saving their gold, I'm managing my capital sustainably, so that I have something to eat when I am grey and old, or choose to invest in something I approve of without losing value by waiting. Based on history, Business will object to many people escaping wage slavery for the same reason that it objected to slaves saving their own gold: our capital (*real* estate), our resources and labour—is aggregating outside of their economy and control. It's not in my interest to suggest how Business might prevent a Deliberate Revolution.

In arising through a new conceptual space as Business once arose between aristocrats and serfs, it is also possible that a Deliberate Revolution succeeds. Whether or not people will cooperate to create Deliberate Corporations, or even a Deliberate Government, is not up to me alone. There is no reason to suppose that a desirable, technologically advanced society could not continue to evolve on the basis of educated citizens who worked 10 to 20 hours a week on projects that require social cooperation, making quality products with lasting use value, and spend the rest of their time looking after their personal needs and enjoying family, leisure and learning. Less work and less resources for a better lifestyle works for me.

Part 2: Stabbing the Chimera

It was never my intention to provide an *encyclopedia* of Deliberate living, with chapters on gardening, storing, building, solar power, and so on, but to present Deliberate Economics as a rational alternative to wage slavery. My methods are evolving and may come out of date, or apply to the wrong climate. Maybe you have a better way. I'm thinking that if you found this book, you know how to find these instructions, and which you need first. For most urban dwellers, that's learning how to cook.

If sounds like a lot to learn, take solace in the fact that these were everyday skills mastered by teenagers at one time. Adequate results are usually achieved after one or two tries, and then you get better. Few people have my experience of living both ways. They focus on elements of my story that remind us of homesteaders struggling to survive: we have access to technologies that did not exist in the past, not even for Business Owners. I'm thinking a car or truck, a chainsaw, table-top flour mills, LED lights, solar power, water pumps, insulation, communications technologies, air-tight wood stoves.... These relatively inexpensive technologies make the prospect of a Deliberate life today both easier and less isolating than it would have been in the past. Population density makes isolation hard to find, even if you want it. We are comparing what we can get for a day's work now with what else we can get for a day's work now.

There are some common places to save labour and resources while creating use value, however, conversations that keep coming up. First of these is understanding the economics of consumer conveniences, from food to credit cards and loyalty programs. Next, we turn to practical alternatives to personal care products, such as soap and laundry detergent, along with details about why this switch matters to your health as much as your pocketbook. As growing food is a primary theme, I will talk about gardening the Forest Way, or gardening without digging the soil or adding chemical inputs. This approach is gaining credibility worldwide, and addresses concerns we may have about the labour required, or whether machinery is desired.

2.1 Purchased Food & Consumer Conveniences

Looking back, these seeds were planted when I was a graduate student, then living off a scholarship in an apartment in Kingston, Ontario. A condition of that scholarship was that I not be employed more than 10 hours a week, and those 10 hours were filled by a Teaching Assistantship. Making other wage-slave agreements was forbidden. Hmm. This economic structure made it tempting to take student loans. In the news, Banks were complaining about the Government forcing them to give student loans and accept the interest. I demonstrated my sympathy with their plight by not-taking a student loan for food. Trading exercise-time for gardening-time didn't violate scholarship conditions. Fortunately, the landlord was comfortable with me digging up some of the yard, as long as I did not allow the garden to become an eyesore. It was my first go at gardening and storing food, successful despite many beginner errors. I remember preparing a 6'x6' area for tomatoes and putting away over 60 litres from that small patch, and having fresh salads half the year from the rest. I wasn't accumulating money yet, and the Bank may have not have appreciated my sympathy. But I could buy other necessities inside my budget without more debt, and left a student diet behind. More efficient, more humane.

Economically, when you buy food, you are buying people's labour. Food is free of cost, like other resources, but access requires social power, and players in the chain from farm to table demand their profit. In some cases, plantation slavery is still the source of labour. Many are surprised to learn about 8 prosecutions for slavery in *this* century, on Florida tomato farms. These farms supplied tomatoes for McDonald's, Burger King,

Wendy's, Mr. Submarine, and the hard tasteless tomatoes sold during the winter in Northern US States and Canada (B. Esterbrook, *Tomatoland*, 2011). Wage slaves have no idea what makes burgers affordable.

I digress; the point is that, if you're hurting for money already, perhaps underemployed, you make your own economic situation worse by hiring or enslaving someone to grow your food, can or freeze for you, throwing around social power like a Business Owner. The quality of the food available has consequences to your health. Bad health is expensive, painful, and hard on relationships, which leads to bad health.... So cooking is the first and most-accessible place to start a Deliberate life. Next is buying in bulk directly from farmers at harvest time, while learning to store and grow your own food. Buying directly minimizes costs and maximizes the information you have about what you eat.

A significant change over this last century is the extent to which wage slaves have turned to convenience foods. Economically, carrots that you still have to cook are a convenience, because you did not grow or harvest them, but paid for that labour. If we were doing this as a form of social cooperation whereby each and all benefit from participating, then that benefit would be there in our savings, or in the increasing value of wages or reduced labour hours, but it's not.

Products we call 'conveniences' appear to save time and labour, but they don't actually do so for wage slaves. Instead they re-arrange labour in time, moving it to a time that is "more convenient" for some reason. It takes more labour hours, overall, to create this apparent efficiency. Thoreau noticed this about using work-horses on farms. The work horse didn't save the farmer work overall, because it needed to be fed all winter and housed all year, but there were key times, like spring ploughing, when it could do specialized work in a short time. Grabbing fast food on the way home, you know that it would be cheaper and healthier to cook something, more efficient and more humane. But in that moment you're stressed and tired, looking to turn cooking-time into eating- and resting-time, so that you'll be fed and ready to work tomorrow. You'll be spared the inconvenience of growing, harvesting and cooking, in exchange for wages, or your most productive work hours, if you spend *extra* wages to create the convenience, plus some profit.

Conveniences are by design to the advantage of Business Owners rather than consumers. By feeding and housing a horse all year, the farmer reaps the convenience of having it ready when work needs to be done. When you buy ready-made food, Business reaps the convenience of having you ready when work needs to be done. The horse pays for winter hay and housing by ploughing. You pay Business for food and housing from your wages, which come from your labour. Both are in this situation because of the job, their slavery. So *the convenience is an employment cost*. If you spend all of your wages, necessity keeps you coming to work. It doesn't really matter to your employer if either your job or this food you're eating is likely to kill you; ideally, something will before you start collecting your pension.

Once a convenience is socially normalized, fulfilling the chimera's expectation makes work rather than saves it, thereby multiplying the losses involved in re-arranging time and creating profit. Conveniences then become labour-makers.

When the washing machine was introduced, for example, it seemed that it would save time compared to hand-washing clothes. At the time a worker would have a couple of sets of work clothes that were worn threadbare before replacement; children's clothes were sewn from flour sacks and other remnants of cloth; and many had an outfit they wore to formal occasions, and kept clean. However, once washing machines became part of the middle-class chimera, so did owning more clothes and expecting them to be cleaner, whiter. More workers wore Business clothes. The outcome of normalizing this convenience was more unpaid work—mostly for women—not less, and more waste from the clothing industry, because the chimera requires workers to replace good clothes in response to fashion trends and Business literally burns tonnes of unsold new clothing every year to make way for more.

More recently, computers and cell phones made it possible to check messages at any time. At first, relatively few had access. The convenience has been normalized, so many employers give you the phone at their expense to make sure you have it when they want you, thus more ordinary wage slaves are never really "off" work.

Incidentally, I have yet to own a cell phone. When I grew up, we went to work, school, camping, shopping, fishing, skiing, out for dinner, you name it, without one, and never thought we were risking our lives in doing so. Devices called *pagers* existed, that would beep and show a phone number to call. Doctors and drug dealers had them, maybe Politicians. I never thought of myself as that important, and both the Oasis Project and my current home are in locations where cell service is spotty. Readers outside Canada should know that we have the worst, most expensive cell service in the world, should this utility seem advantageous where you are. I am sometimes confronted with, "What will you do if you break down on the road?" Well, it happened, but in rural Ontario after 30 seconds of waving at traffic, the 5th car to pass stopped, and Buddy said, "I had to stop, seeing all those cars go by you on such a hot day!" He had to drive 15 minutes to get reception to call a tow truck, however, so if I'd had a cell phone that day, I'd have been flagging down traffic anyway. Estimating $500 a year for the 30 years since the chimera required them, I haven't spent $15 000 on cell phones so far. I will admit, as one who advocates straddling two economies, that this takes advantage of the fact that everyone next to me has a cell phone. Herd immunity.

This next step is a little complicated but helps complete the pattern of value extraction through conveniences. Remember that money is just one commodity among others and that the exchange values of commodities are changing all the time but not their use values. So money is a commodity, wood is, wheat, housing.... Some of these commodities are conveniences, labour savers that become labour makers, and so avenues for value extraction. Like washing machines and cell phones.

Now, recognize that "credit" is a commodity. You can buy and sell debts. The way to expand this business is to create more debts, to buy and sell and collect interest from. Not so long ago, the common wisdom was *credit is for things that make money*, which means that credit was used to enable production. Credit would only be extended for buying or making things whose value increased, a house or factory, in order to guarantee repayment. If all your business is is you, a wage slave, it might make sense to borrow for land to live from or a house that you'll pay off so you don't pay rent. If you are a construction company, you might borrow money for heavy equipment. These are investments you'd expect to make money from. But even a car to get you to work is a declining asset; it was a questionable use of credit at one time, and still is from a Business perspective. Again, credit existed and was defended as necessary because it enabled production.

Credit cards introduced the idea of credit for consumption: cars, food, clothes, vacations, gifts... whatever. Things that lose most of their market value the moment you buy them, rather than assets acquiring value after you build them. Credit is being used here as a convenience. This was not less work than using cash: when they first came out, people pulling out cards took longer at the checkout line than cash customers because they had to show ID and sign a little form, then they had to track and pay the same bill again. Credit cards are a convenience that enables consumption, unlike traditional credit that enables production. Like other consumer conveniences, they re-arrange time such that consumption comes before production, and invite you to consume money, or time, that you don't have at all. Credit cards look like capitalism's answer to the paradox of time travel, but they are just as likely to destroy your future. While some pay it off every month, the average Canadian carries over $8000 in revolving consumer debt (as does the average American, but in $US). "It's there for when you need it", a man I know used to say, before going bankrupt, twice.

We're encouraged to do it with loyalty programs that give you points the more you use your credit card, so people are using credit cards for consumption in the grocery store and at the gas station. Loyalty programs were the *first* Social Media, before email or Google (the company). Where Media is a business that sells audiences to other businesses, Social Media is a business that sells audiences' social information to other businesses. Today, the credit-card companies won't allow retailers to offer different prices for cash customers, but insist on their percentage in proportion to the points granted by the card, and our updated Privacy Agreements state clearly that we no longer have a choice about keeping our data private. Loyalty programs create added burdens to the entire consumer market, charging us in exchange for "loyalty points," which are far more flexible than fiat money. But credit as a convenience, 'there for when you need it," ropes in a lot of value from mystified workers, who are able to spend more than the surplus cash in their pocket and as a rule, do, often fulfilling the details of the middle-class chimera.

That's convenient, for creditors.

2.2 Soap and Laundry: The Big Cover-Up:

In 2017, the average Canadian household spent just over $1300 on personal-care products. This is why, and how, I got that under $20.

Typically, a person puts on at least 5 artificial fragrances every morning: in soap, shampoo, conditioner, shaving gel, armpit goo. Extra cologne or after shave and scented laundry detergent make it easy to wear 7– 8 with scented dryer sheets, 9 with an air-freshener, 10+ if you pick up scents from products used to clean the sink and floor. Make-up, cosmetics and lotions add a fragrance with each product, in order to cover the scent of rancid fat and chemicals. No one is regulating the safety of these products or can even be sure of their ingredients, because regulations would be bad for Business. Long lists of formally banned products are no reason to suppose legal products are desirable. There are abundant reasons, from a health perspective, to avoid eating detergents, artificial fragrances, and pesticides.

Yes, I said *eating*. A condition of obtaining a permit to buy and use agricultural pesticides is knowing that our skin is the largest organ of our body. Some parts absorb up to 100% of organic compounds and organic solvents on contact. These are our armpits, face, scalp, eyes, nasal passages/lungs, palms, crotch, and the soles of our feet—all the places where personal-care products go, along with their preservatives and antibiotics (pesticides), and fragrances. If you can smell something, you're eating it and breathing it in. This is necessarily true, since nasal receptors work by capturing particles in the air and sending some electricity through them, and each smell is a product of the electrical resistance of each kind of particle. Arsenic and almonds smell the same because their electrical resistance is the same, though that is where the similarity ends. Logically, body care products ought to be edible because people "eat" them through their skin and lungs to use them, like when we wear a nicotine patch or smoke. Even if you're just walking down the aisle at a store and can smell the scented cat litter, for example, this is evidence of a packaging failure that puts you at risk.

It is astonishing to me how often I have this conversation and people say "I don't smell anything. My nose is always stuffed." Why is that?

I remember the first day in the shower that I stopped to question doing the same. Many of my days were spent just sitting. You don't literally "sweat-out" an essay or report while "working in your field", so I became curious about why I was using these products as directed on the label. In hindsight, it was because the chimera said that I was ugly and smelly, and that these products would make me attractive and fragrant, so I needed them to fit-in, or date. It's no more absurd than when Richard Overton sued Anheuser-Busch because no girls in bikinis appeared when he opened their beer on the beach, instead of thinking about the ingredients in the beer.

Armpit Goo—deodorant or anti-perspirant—is not necessary, even harmful. We sweat saltwater, and from areas that grow hair, a little fat. These have no smell. The bacteria that live on skin and their by-products do. If you bathe every day or so, there won't be any smells, because you rinse off most of the bacteria, as well as any fat or dead skin that would feed them. This does mean staying in the shower or tub long enough to exfoliate. Depending on the work you do, you may be cleaner taking a long bath every few days than a quick shower every day, so that you exfoliate properly, and not sully your clothing as quickly as a result. It confounds the middle-class chimera to say so. Armpit goo introduces new food to your skin, even though the product may contain antibiotics. This is the sludge that remains in your armpits after the product has "stopped working". Your body may try to sweat extra just to wash it out of your pores. This sludge will feed different bacteria than used to live there, creating new unwanted smells, making you want to wash and put on more goo. It may stain your clothes. Maybe you even think you, personally, have some unique odour problem related to your nature rather than your products. Dermatologists say only 1% to 2% of us sweat extra, but this begins unscented like anyone else's. I have not put anything in my armpits for decades, and there have been no complaints about bad smells, and no stains. Simple savings here.

Shampoo is sort of addictive, because your scalp adapts to it. Detergents strip the oil from your hair, making your scalp adapt by producing more oil, so you think your hair is greasy and wash it again. A vicious circle that sells shampoo and conditioner well. A few weeks of washing with just water breaks the addiction. As a man with thinning hair I was comfortable shaving it and starting over, washing only with home-made soap since, and it doesn't get greasy anymore. If you do a little research, you will find people with beautiful hair that never sees shampoo, or others who make their own hair soap. People form similarly addictive-adaptive relationships with lip balm and skin moisturizers, where the body adapts to the extra oils and waxes by making less, making you think YOU are a dry person and need these products.

Some olive or coconut oil works here, if you need an occasional moisturizer.

I began making soap after my favourite brand changed the recipe. I had started to get itchy after a shower, because the new product was detergent, not soap, with artificial fragrances instead of cedar oil. I learned that except for handmade, most "soap" on the market these days is actually detergent. This includes most "natural" or "green" cleaning products containing sodium laurel sulphate—the same detergent as in regular products that one is buying "green" or "natural" to avoid, but at a premium price. It shows up on labels under a few other names: sulfuric acid monododecyl ester sodium salt, sodium salt, hydrogen sulfate, dodecyl alcohol, sodium dodecanesulfate, and sodium monododecyl sulfate.

"Natural" means only that there are no ghosts in the package, nothing "supernatural", guaranteed. The chimera is on the package, not in it.

Soap is what you get when you mix lye (sodium hydroxide or potassium hydroxide) with fat or oil and then heat it—a third thing that forms. Soap is hydrophobic (repels water) at one side of the molecule and hydrophilic (sticks to water) on the other, which means that it gets between you and the oil on your skin when mixed with water, letting the dirt and body oil slide off in the form of soap scum. It is often referred to as a surfactant because of this ability to break the surface tension of water, and essentially make water wetter. Soap is usually used with pesticides for this reason: it helps the pesticide stick.

People used to get the lye by leaching ashes in water, and then boiling down the leachate. You were done boiling when it floated a fresh-laid egg and stripped the quills off a chicken feather dipped for 2 to 3 seconds. These tests were fallible and did not account for impurities. If you added too much lye, then the extra would remain after converting the fat to soap and burn your skin; if you add too little, or impurities made it too weak, then there is too much oil or fat left over, and you have a sloppy, greasy mess. That was how it turned out for me when I tried it the old way. Given these options, I guess people tended to make it too strong rather than too weak, and lye soap is remembered as a harsh product.

We have soap calculators today—apps you can download— that calculate the correct amount of lye for a given amount of each type of fat or oil. We can also buy manufactured lye, which is cheap and more importantly, consistent. The result is whatever kind of soap you like, predictably, as long as you measure ingredients by weight. It's just cooking. I made a recipe satisfactory for all purposes—shower, shave, what's left of my hair. It costs under $20 and takes about 3 hours, including clean-up, to make a 7 pound batch of soap, unscented, and while I sell enough to pay for the ingredients, for the most part it is gifts and personal use for a year. If we count the revenue from sales and small gifts I don't have to buy, I make enough on this one to show a small profit.

One friend's cat ate an entire bar with no ill effects, which suggests that the old practice of washing a child's mouth out with soap was merely unpleasant, rather than dangerous as it would be with a detergent bar today, and it meets the edibility standard suggested for body care products. I don't think that it tastes good though, nor do I recommend animal testing. We just learned that he had to hide this soap from that cat. My cats are not interested. My tenant likes it during deer season because the scent in other products tips off the deer. Another friend uses it for all purposes, like me, and credits it with allowing a skin condition to heal.

Zieba's Soap

I use a hot process and superfat 3%.
900g coconut oil
600g olive oil, low quality
600g sunflower oil
600g beef tallow; I render my own
400g sodium hydroxide lye added to 1026 grams water in a
Pyrex dish and mixed well—it gets hot

Abundant information exists about hot-process soap, so I won't repeat details of soap making here you can find easily. But if you put all of this (or 1/2 of everything for a smaller batch —fill no more than half the pot that you use) into a slow cooker and simmer it for a few of hours, stirring occasionally, until it looks like dirty Vaseline, and then put it hot into a mold, you'll have soap to carve into bars when it cools.

It seems to me, as far as good manners go, that I am doing my guests a favour by providing a healthy, unscented soap, rather than adding another fragrance, real or artificial, to their olfactory collage. Insisting that they wear the scent that I chose, or not wash their hands at all, is just that.

Laundry detergent does not usually list its ingredients, but is advertised to be a mix of detergents, enzymes to break down proteins, and little bits of plastic that work as abrasives, and some powerful artificial fragrances, which often leak out of the box. Once these fragrances touch your clothes, it can be difficult to find anything to wear to go to the hospital or other 'scent free' environment. Clothes need to be washed and dried in the sun 3 times to remove these products. Hot water and bleach are helpful. Running the washer empty first with a cup of bleach on a hot setting should get most of the residue out: otherwise clothes will just re-acquire more fragrance from the machine.

The recipe below is widely circulated online; it uses soap to break water tension, and washing soda and borax to do the cleaning. It costs $2 to $3 for 5 gallons. You can buy a bar of laundry soap pretty cheap, or, make your own.

Either way, grate a bar of laundry soap into a large pot. Add water, heat and stir until the soap has dissolved. Pour the hot liquid into a 5-gallon pail. Add more hot water, a cup of washing soda and a cup of borax, and stir to dissolve. Bring the water level up to 4 or 5 gallons in the bucket. Stir until uniform, and then let it sit, you're done.

Use from the pail or put it in smaller containers. In the morning, you will have a slimy gel similar to the laundry detergent that you pay for. Shake/stir before using as there are no emulsifiers here. Borax and washing soda aren't edible, but I have not heard of any adverse reactions. Lately, I've been making just 1/4 of the recipe at a time, in a used vinegar jug, enough for 48 loads.

I have learned that 1/4cup per load is enough to clean dirty farm clothes: too much does not rinse out properly, and it is important to clean your washer periodically by running it empty with a cup of bleach. Both using the right amount of soap and cleaning the machine are recommended by machine manufacturers regardless of what kind of detergent you use, in order to ensure that the machine is clean of residues and that there is no mould hiding in seals. After a while these residues will sully clothes rather than clean them, creating bad smells, and in some cases foster harmful bacteria and viruses. Hot water works better because bacteria don't like hot water. I learned these things by putting too much soap in, maybe because it seemed free, and I suppose these details explain why this recipe works really well for some people and not so well for others.

It may sound contrary to environmental concerns to recommend going back to washing clothes and even rinsing them in hot or warm water. I believe that the practice comes out ahead. No abrasive micro plastics as are in commercial products means that there are none to go into the environment or abrade fibres, so your clothes last longer. Also, by not using commercial products, you're not getting a new plastic container every time. Washing soda and borax are also easier on your fibres and septic than cold-water detergents, fragrances and enzymes. It's a fix if commercial products give you a rash. A problem I am encountering is that you cannot find a new washing machine for sale that has a hot-water rinse, if you want one. New washers meet Energy Star requirements (remember, Government makes laws that look socially progressive...) by using electronic sensors that limit the entry of hot water, so are designed to sell commercial detergents that work in these machines, and to wear out clothes faster, and to make it difficult to clean diapers at home, pressuring people to buy disposable. All convenient.

That's not to say that this recipe doesn't work with a warm wash and cold rinse available, just that I'd like the option of hot water, and it disturbs me that washers are precisely designed to prevent me from controlling water temperature in any way. Sometimes we want to sanitize. If your clothes are particularly dirty, add more washing soda and/or borax to the load (it goes on the bottom of a top-loader before your clothes, to dissolve best) but not more laundry soap, since the role of the soap is to break the surface tension of the water, and we aren't adding more water; the soda and borax, or bleach at times, are the cleaners. Some people add essential oil, like pine, cedar or lavender. I find that much of it washes away or cooks out in a dryer or in the sun, and so instead, place essential oils into my dresser where the clothes are stored, or dab some on for special occasions. More scent remains using less essential oil, which is either expensive, or work to produce at home.

When I was a child, the "problem" of **static cling** was invented, in order to sell dryer sheets and other anti-static products, which then became part of the middle-class chimera. TV commercials showed a woman walking on a downtown street with a mans' sock clinging to the back of her skirt—an invitation for men in the street to stare at her derrière. Oops. Nobody noticed that men's socks and women's skirts wouldn't go in the same load, or that static cling is just not powerful enough to last that long. It dissipates in a few minutes. If it really bothers you, add a foil ball to the dryer. Better, use a clothesline and gain some anti-bacterial and whitening action from the sun. Anti-static products add an alkalizing electrolyte layer to your clothes in order to dissipate static charges, leaving electrolyte on your clothes, and maybe your skin: sweat and dead skin are slightly acidic, and the electrolyte is alkaline, so they'll react when you sweat. Your clothes won't stick to each other, but dust/detritus will stick to them, and to you.

A **fabric softener** may be part of the anti-static sheet, or liquid fabric softeners are added during the rinse cycle of the wash. Fabric softener is oil that coats your clothes, so they feel slick. Slick is sort of like soft, like the difference between a wet cat and a dry cat. It goes in during the rinse cycle, or as a dryer sheet, because washing removes oils. Fabric oiling makes towels less absorbent because oil repels water. It provides a base for dirt and detritus to stick to on all of your clothes, so you'll need to wash them, and yourself, more often. Slick. We don't need it at all. If you have a container in your washer for fabric softener introduced in the rinse cycle, a little vinegar in there instead will help as a rinsing agent, particularly for hard water.

Laundry Blue.   Before leaving the laundry, one more thing to expect when you either make your own laundry detergent or just purchase one *that has no dye in it:* on the one hand, home made detergent is easier on fabrics because it has no microplastic abrasives or cold-water enzymes, so your clothes will last longer, but on the other, longer-lasting whites will not stay as white. It is because whites aren't actually white: they are blue. You can see this when you hang (new) white clothes or sheets in the sun: there is a distinctly blue hue. This is because light-blue looks whiter to our eyes, particularly when the alternative is a light grey or beige, the natural colour of the fabric. It looks whiter with some blue in it than if you bleached alone. At one time, "laundry blue", or copper sulphate, was added to laundry, and today, most laundry detergent has blue dye in it. Without dye and with a longer useful life, the natural colour of your fibres, whites in particular, will start to show through. A stab in the chimera's back, unless you mistake the colour change for worn-out fabric.

Perhaps the most over-priced item in the bathroom is the **disposable razor**. They have coatings on them to make them glide well when new, but these wash off quickly, and soap scum can build up on the blades. Try stropping your disposable razor when it feels dull. You may have seen, in movies or sometimes still in reality, a barber "stropping" a straight-razor on a leather strap just before shaving with it, to refine the edge. With a disposable razor, first clean and dry the razor. Get an old pair of jeans, canvas, or the back of an old leather belt. Run the dry razor in the direction of the blades, rather than against them as when shaving. Run it lightly across the material about 20 times. This will hone the blade, remove burrs, and polish the exposed surface. If you search this topic, you'll find pictures, videos, and variations. My last disposable razor lasted 3 years this way, considering it as sharp as long as I could get a good shave and have no irritation afterwards (with no "after-shave" lotion). It does feel different once the original goo is gone: it feels like razors always felt before the goo was added, and so this difference should not be interpreted as the razor being dull. I decided to take a new one out of the package when I moved, so I don't know how much more than 3 years they last.

Budget time: what do you spend every year on laundry, soap, shampoo, razors, etc.? I've got it under $20. I have not addressed cosmetics, which the chimera demands particularly of women, although these too can be made at home or their necessity re-evaluated. I also have not discussed cutting my own hair instead of paying for that service.

2.3 Prohibition Tax: Weed, Alcohol, and Tobacco

For economic purposes, I assume that if you drink, or smoke, or toke, you're going to continue. Many regard their substances as necessities. Along with opium, these were viable options for home businesses at one time, because the best products can only be produced by hand. Prohibition and taxation fixed that problem, from a Business perspective, adding their inflated price to GDP.

As a result, a package of cigarettes a day, in Canada, is $15, or over $5000 a year. A third of our market, determined by examining cigarette butts in public ashtrays, buys cigarettes from a Reserve at half price or less, with quality issues at the bottom end and some chemical-free products at the top. Treaties say goods made and sold on the Reserve bear no tax, and Business complaining about competition has the Government say that cigarettes made and sold on the Reserve are illegal because they haven't been taxed. Tobacco you grew is OK.

You can see where this is going. For comparison, tomatoes take twice as much room in the garden as tobacco, or the space needed to produce a few pounds of beans in a good year. Good luck trading a few pounds of beans for a year's tobacco. Homegrown tobacco is free, as well as free of chemicals. These are introduced as pesticides from the seedling stage, and as hormones used to prevent branches from developing. Other chemicals are introduced during processing. Literally hundreds of them. Real tobacco takes some getting used to, in the sense that some of these chemicals, like food-grade anti-freeze, made the nicotine preserved by other chemicals get into your lungs and bloodstream faster, so there is a rush that's missing. While I have no experience here, I understand eager people inject opiates into their veins or put LSD in their eyeballs, rather than eat them, precisely to get a "rush" from all of the drug hitting their system at once, and so I think that the chemicals in commercial tobacco that are responsible for the nicotine rush also make it more addictive. The same food-grade anti-freeze is the basis of nicotine solutions used by electronic cigarettes. I don't notice so much now when I'm spending time somewhere I can't smoke for a few hours, and I smoke substantially less.

A case of beer a week, $40 for the budget brands, is over $2000 a year. You can cut the costs of beer and wine in half with beer kits or wine kits, and work down from there as you move away from kits and learn to cook with raw ingredients. At one time, I got a deal on a pail of malt and made beer for 8 cents a bottle. You can buy distillation equipment made for essential oils and distilling water, but are not supposed to distil alcohol from your beer or wine with it. Chances are, however, that if you make some ethanol (as lamp fuel of course) and refrained from sharing it widely or selling it to minors, the police wouldn't be on your doorstep: it is a Federal Tax law you're violating (Al Capone went down for tax evasion), not something local police are paid to police. This law has nothing to do with real concerns about selling uncontrolled liquor, or knowing how to separate the methanol so you don't go blind or die.

A quarter-ounce of cannabis a week, at a legal average around $10/gram, is $70/week or $3640 a year. Free-market prices can be half or double, depending on where you live, but where they are double it is still illegal to grow your own. Your weed can be free, and in my experience is the easiest of the three as far as producing a satisfactory product goes. The plant on the back cover produced over 2 pounds. There is a similar deal about selling it, whether growing is legal or not in your area, but the penalties are more serious than for violating tax laws relating to tobacco or alcohol.

I know of a couple who drinks a case of 24 beer and smoke a pack of cigarettes a day, each. That's $50 000 a year if you do the math. They live in a trailer parked in a friend's driveway. The Government argued that using taxes to create prohibition prices for these products would foster their health, and it failed. It made them broke, taking advantage of their addictions as the chimera takes advantage of any need or desire, and so guaranteed that they need their jobs. While this couple represents an extreme, we all know people who have spent enough on these products to be free of debt otherwise. Most of the lost cash went to taxes. The result is what prohibitive taxation was said to avoid: poor choices in food, health care, warm clothing, or credit, because the money has to come from somewhere. A moderate consumer can easily rack up $2000 a year here, which translates to over $2500 of after-tax income for a wage slave. After 10 years, that's $25 000 in real savings.

2.4 Forest Way Farming

For centuries, we thought that it was necessary to dig a garden every year. People have been fed this way for a long time, just as many continue to be fed using slash-and-burn techniques to clear land. But these methods deplete soil fertility, cause topsoil erosion, and contribute to illusions that growing food is more work than buying it with wages, or that it needs machinery and Government subsidies.

Most agree that a 1/4 acre or less, roughly 100 feet square, can be worked by hand. Historically and in much of the world today, 2 acres are managed at the family level. This work is less onerous than it may sound. We tend to imagine ourselves as commercial farmers who need to work a field at once and plant one crop in it. So we think "tiller" rather than "tractor" is the right accommodation to our scale. However, since we are planting a wide variety of crops which go in at different times over the course of spring and summer, a smaller area can be prepared and planted at a time. It's better for the soil that way, and easier to do by hand. While backyard gardeners often "put the garden in" on a weekend, this is to accommodate their job, at the expense of planting each crop at the most beneficial time for that crop.

Let's go back to the need to dig every year. We used to think the purpose was to loosen the soil and improve its structure, to introduce and mix nutrients, and to kill weeds. I even remember double-digging beds, which means going down a second depth of your digging fork to loosen the subsoil. I thought that I was permanently improving a larger root zone. Now we know that when we turn soil, we introduce extra oxygen, which fosters aerobic bacteria, and thus accelerates the decomposition of organic matter. The organic material is decomposing faster than our crop can consume the nutrients released in the process, so the difference is wasted soil fertility. That's because nutrients are only available in the ion forms plants can take up during a phase of decomposition. If these ions are not taken up by plants, they leach out in rain, go into the air, or bind with other elements in the soil. Tilling also leaves soil bare, exposed to sun and wind erosion. We also cut through mushroom networks, the fungal mycelium that live in the soil. Fungi are the primary decomposers of cellulose, or the woody parts of dead plants and roots, and our mulch. Our soil needs fungi to be healthy, as well as predatory insects and toads whose homes are disturbed by tilling. Turning soil was actually doing harm, and adding a burden.

7 years ago, I began farming the Forest Way after reading the work of Masanobu Fukuoka, a farmer who made a living without equipment in Japan. He developed a wheat-rice rotation in which one crop was planted into the stubble and mulched with the straw of the last. His grandson continues on the same land with the same approach, which I found adaptable to my climate and crops in Canada, and in Sierra Leone, where high rainfall and acid soil mean chemical fertilizers don't work at all. Given these geographic extremes (Japan, Canada, West Africa) the method works anywhere there could be farmable soil, including on slopes and ridges where tractors cannot go.

Forests have great soil. That's why Business is eager to cut them or burn them down for farming, regarding the wood and the fertility as free, economically. Nobody cultivated that soil to make it, so there was no cost for labour. Forest ecosystems created deep, fertile soil by themselves. This fertility was the economic windfall presented by the New World at one time, why it was worth pioneers' trouble to start over. Leaves and branches fall, animals and insects chew them up, live and die, worms and other insects come to the surface and drag material down bit by bit, roots grow deeper over time and decompose deeper as a result. So the soil in an old-growth forest, or virgin prairie, already has a better texture and fertility than we can create by tilling, a result of the plants, insects and small animals that are parts of it. Fungal mycelium gives soil sponge-like qualities that hold a balance between too much and too little water. Fungi have been recently recognized as having symbiotic relationships with plants, functioning as information and nutrient highways, and at times controlling disease directly. Fertile soil is this ecosystem all living together, not sterile dirt. We cut that up when we till, and we expose it to erosion and drying in the sun if we don't keep it covered with mulch.

Forest Way farming is less work. We just stop digging, and apply mulch and compost materials from the top. These materials would be gathered anyway. The few weeds that make it through are lanky and easy to pick. This addresses concerns that we may have about the labour involved in turning soil or weeding. We see at the same time that machines that dig soil are conveniences. Farmers who buy them must produce more to pay for them, thus bringing down the market value of their own product, making more work for themselves, and making it seem uneconomical for you to feed yourself.

The relationship between farm machinery and Forest Way farming is like two economies that cannot mesh. Preparing a field for tractor or even horse-driven implements requires levelling, and removing all stumps and stones, and then replacing this fertility from another source. Even small mechanical seeders will operate only with soil that is flat, smooth, uniform, and cleared of mulch: dead. No-till seed drills used by AgriBusiness can deal with a small quantity of leftover mulch from stubble, but are unable to work through a mulch that is thick-enough to control weeds and fertilize the crop, so are designed to operate with herbicide sprays. We address the illusions of purchased chemical fertilizer and herbicides at the same time.

My soil improved from not-tilling it—just adding compost and mulch to the top at the usual rate. A clear difference showed up after a year. When I had been digging every year, the beds would be fluffed up high after preparation, but flat again by the following spring. When I stopped digging, they stopped going flat. More organic material stayed in the soil, banked more nutrients (less oxygen, less decomposition), and supported a better texture. Mushrooms were popping up everywhere.

Once a garden is mulched, either digging or tilling areas within it requires you to move that mulch aside. If you till a mulch in before it is finished compost, the woody bits of the mulch will tie up the nitrogen in your soil until they decompose—something that doesn't happen when decomposition occurs naturally on top of the soil. There are no machines that will move mulch aside and put it back afterwards, without mixing it with soil.

As an experiment, I began a 400 square foot garden in an area where small trees and bushes had moved into the grass. Preparing new ground for machinery, rather than for farming, requires stumps and roots to be pulled out of the soil rather than be left in place to decompose as fertilizer. Preparing new ground for growing food can much less work, if you let nature take its course.

I cut all at ground level and piled it, along with other branches pruned that year. This produced a brush pile that was 5 or 6 feet high, that had to go somewhere anyway. It was mostly in place where it fell. This material smothered the soil, rather than adding oxygen to it. After 3 years' doing nothing, the pile was under a foot high. I removed the remaining big pieces, leaving the small crumble as mulch, and planted beans and potatoes through it. I had not dug the soil ever, had not removed stumps or roots, or any rocks that were not directly in my way when I planted. Absolute minimum effort. Yields were lower the first year, and then as good as the old garden space. Under these conditions, slowly decomposing roots tied up nitrogen the first year, but when they did decompose, they provided nutrition tunnels that guided new roots—from my crop—deeper into the soil.

Carrots are the exception (literally, this time), in terms of needing worked soil; even their much larger relative, the parsnip, is fine on its own. I plant carrots immediately after garlic is harvested, in the same bed; garlic needs to be lifted by hand, so you effectively hand-dug that bed anyway, just at the right time to plant carrots for fall and winter harvest. Potatoes need some help (digging) in heavy clay soil, until its condition has improved. In my rotation, fall-planted garlic follows potatoes harvested in August, which again means that the soil was disturbed by a harvest process already. But the rest—corn, beans, tomatoes, peppers, cucumbers and squash, greens, onions, brassicas, grains—they didn't seem to notice I stopped digging, and yields improved with the condition of the soil. As you rotate crops, you wind up disturbing it all every so many years a bit at a time for these roots, but it's a long way from digging every year and cultivating during the growing season.

During the last few years, I have been employing cover crops, or crops planted with the intention of letting them die there, to build soil fertility. For example, as potato beds become available in August (one bed goes to garlic), there is still a fair bit of growing season left. Mulch was pushed aside to lift the potatoes in order to prevent mixing mulch with soil. At that moment there is an opportunity to choose between spending a few minutes pushing mulch back (at the end of the season there will be less of it, mixing with some soil each time you move it), or spending a few minutes dropping some seeds into the loose soil. Bare soil is bad. Planting something in the soil means that we scavenge nutrients for the rest of the growing season, nutrients that would otherwise be lost. In the past, many would choose a nitrogen-fixing legume here, however, the accounting shows that a plant that grows large quickly scavenges more nitrogen and other nutrients in its mass than a slow-growing bean.

I plant broom corn, a kind of sorghum used to make brooms. A small bed provides free seeds. Planted thickly by scattering and raking on the loose soil or even into a thin mulch, the broom corn comes up like a lawn, preventing weeds from sprouting. When it gets to be 3 feet tall, I trim it to a foot in order to prevent stalks from getting too woody, and to spur more root growth. Trimming happens once before frost kills it. It then lies down under the snow, providing mulch for the winter and a loose, mostly weed-free bed for spring planting; just push the straw aside. This fall, I dropped freshly gathered leaves into the standing straw, before snow laid it down, and the straw held the leaves in place against fall winds. This was no more work than dropping the same leaves in a pile, and it will result in soil that is ready-to-go in spring.

These little activities make more efficient use of labour and resources, and are more humane, than messing with a power tiller, when we're talking about 1/4 acre.

Part 3: A Capitalist's Critique of Capitalism: Paths and Perspectives

Before you embark on any path ask the question: Does this path have a heart? If the answer is no, you will know it, and then you must choose another path. The trouble is nobody asks the question; and when a man finally realizes that he has taken a path without a heart, the path is ready to kill him. At that point very few men can stop to deliberate, and leave the path. A path without a heart is never enjoyable. You have to work hard even to take it. On the other hand, a path with heart is easy; it does not make you work at liking it.
— Carlos Castaneda, 1968

I've been talking about economics for a long time. Growing up, my family and friends mostly thought that higher education was not for us but for them, so going to University made me a rebel, different, outside. I thought that I was going to learn about a different world, and a better life. That was wrong. I had to learn to see the same world from a different perspective.

Have you ever tried to cut your own hair, guided by your reflection in a mirror? You feel like you're bringing the scissors closer to where you want them, but are actually moving them further away. You can get used to it.

The Business perspective reflects a wage-slave perspective in the same way: the image is perfectly symmetrical, but everything is backwards, right is left and left is right. Inflation is deflation. Growing GDP is good, growing GDP is bad. More consumption is good, more consumption is bad. Capitalism rewards hard work, capitalism takes my hard work away. Your freedom is my slavery. The chimera is a slippery demon. My new university friends talked like we were Business Owners and their good was our good because we were middle class. I found this new view of good and evil perplexing. Once as an undergrad and twice in graduate school, different Professors actually took me aside and told me it was so, to clear my class-confusion. I was a scholar, not working class anymore, and needed to remember that in order to succeed.

This was the twisted reflection in the mirror. In reality, we were all being trained for wage-slave positions, by other wage slaves.

The Cold War (1947–91) was still on, between Capitalism and Socialism, championed by the US and the USSR respectively. "Cold" meant that they did not fire on each other's nations. It was fought through propaganda, a race to develop nuclear and space technologies, and a mix of overt and covert military operations in other nations. It was a war between ideologies. It is fair to say that Market Capitalism was state religion, a kind of social paranoia that came along with this period of economic security. Like a witch in the past, you could get arrested if accused of being a socialist. While long-term detention rarely occurred, you would remain labelled and be blacklisted from many jobs and shunned by the community, maybe beaten, for criticizing market capitalism. At that time, speaking out for the environment, or against drug prohibition, also made you a "left-wing hippie", easy to ignore. President Nixon made marijuana "public enemy number one" in 1971 because he could then arrest young people protesting the Vietnam War; most were pot smokers, so arresting them as criminals eliminated Vietnam protests from the press. Public debate spoke as though Global Capitalism was a chimera, one of socialism's crazy ideas, and as such, had no role in debates, even though globalizing capitalism was the point of the Cold War. It was all about our freedom, our way of life.

By those standards, the celebrated free market economist Adam Smith would have been a socialist, a witch, had he published his defence of a free market just after the Civil War in 1867, when Marx wrote *Das Capital*. Smith and Marx saw the same problem.

Adam Smith wrote *The Wealth of Nations* in 1776, the year the US declared independence. A free market, as Smith understood it, is free of Government intervention. In a Democracy, it is the people who are free, not the state. This is only possible if Government has no democratic authority to manage the economy. A free market means market freedom: no trade deals or import taxes, no flexible currencies, no consumption taxes, no bail outs, no subsidies, no ordering striking workers back to work. Bad business fails, good business succeeds, and individuals decide which is which with their purchasing dollars and the productive activity they choose. A free market economy was managed by the aggregate effect of individual freedom, what Smith called The Invisible Hand — not the Hand of Business Owners. If a free market exists, all that is left for Government to do is administrate public safety: a military to prevent invasion, local police, maybe organize education and health care. If Politicians were allowed to make laws that affect the economy, Smith argued, they would use this power for their own benefit, not for the benefit of the people. Business Owners elected to Government were already doing that. In other words, Smith defended a free market *against* an economy managed by Business Owners. He called our union between Business and Government "Mercantilism" and argued that it was a kind of oppression. It was opposed to democratic freedom and a free market, determining details of people's lives right down to what kind of grape they ate, how much they paid for it, and who got their grape money. During the Cold War, we rebuked the USSR for this level of state authority, called it Totalitarianism.

Which witch is which? To this day, many people think I am some weird kind of socialist. This shared critique on what Smith the free-marketeer called Mercantilism, and what Marx the socialist and the rest of us call Market Capitalism, meant that in the middle-class chimera's view, even a capitalist critique of capitalism was some kind of socialism. Smith predicted a Wealth Gap too, and pointed to it as a measure of inefficiency and injustice.

Where Smith stopped at pointing to Market Capitalism as inefficient and inhumane, Marx saw 60 years later that the Wealth Gap would lead to Global Capitalism's final economic crisis.

That was happening in front of me. Once wages get too low, there is no revenue to come back from sales. Where the Great Depression blamed wage slaves' saved capital for slowing the circulation of money, the flow of money stops in the final crisis because no one has any to buy things with: a few Business Owners have it all. Back then, I beguiled my Business-minded friends by pointing out that the best strategy for an eager socialist is to promote Global Capitalism, indulge every desire they can spend on, and grow the Wealth Gap, to bring on the final crisis... Business Owners were acting like rational socialists. Mirrors work both ways.

It's like playing Monopoly until somebody wins. What happens if we don't finish playing, and leave the game early? I didn't share Marx's prediction of a *violent* revolution when Global Capitalism failed, nor did I see a new set of masters as very revolutionary. Just as we already saw the Wealth Gap rolling towards the final crisis and grinding us up along the way, we already saw that socialism was possessed by a chimera of its own. I wondered about what else rational people might do, and what an end to social oppression of all kinds would look like.

That was 35 years ago. When I talk about Deliberate Economics today, age affects one's perspective on a Deliberate life more than anything else.

Most young adults are struggling to find affordable housing and foresee a laborious and uncertain future, dominated by climate change. They see my life as pretty good by comparison, and the path as accessible. Maybe a way to pursue interests that don't always make money, or just survive.

Older wage slaves already have the most skill, as far as satisfying their needs Deliberately is concerned. These are experienced trades people, farmers, cooks who don't read books or have time for this kind of talk. I've gone to them to learn what to do time and time again, because they know what Business Owners don't know, which is how to do the job.

When I talk about Deliberate Economics with a Bank Director, who endures social pressure to roll with his role, to work and spend on the accoutrements of the Business class, it seems remote. He'll tell me why Deliberate Economics can't work, explains why the money needs to recirculate, why growth is necessary... Business perspective.

As a wage slave, this perspective is telling me I should suck up my increasing personal loss for some general good, like a communist in a society with too little to go around, but the Wealth Gap says otherwise. If Deliberate Economics didn't work, then I would be broke, not free.

Eventually, he will point out that market capitalism wasn't supposed to make people happy. It was supposed to make money. We agree.

This Director and I started this conversation 35 years ago, when we arrived at University and he first tried to explain things to me, like those Professors tried. Don't get me wrong: I needed help seeing other ways.

When the conversation shifts to our perspective as friends and wage slaves, a Bank Director's compensation, like a Professor's, is a fraction of what it was when we chose those paths, thinking the future would be the same. The chimera. Bank Directors enjoyed a second house on a beach in the tropics; Professors got a hot lunch with a beer in the Faculty Lounge. We thought these were positions society respected. It turned out that neither position could afford a housekeeper, or a house in the city, like Archie Bunker could in New York with a blue-collar job. He does not argue that he's better off than me in terms of satisfaction or security, or even money, but that it's too late. We don't talk about how our paths affected our health.

It's the same with most of my middle-aged class, thinking retirement is 10 to 15 years away. Because they still go to work and generate profits for someone else, they're healthy enough to spend less, and given the work that they do, they're smart enough. But I know what is required. If they choose they can't do *any* of it, that becomes reality. Slaying the chimera was a battle of ideas, remember? As an aging parent, not a Bank Director, my old friend sees why his adult children should consider Deliberate Economics in planning their paths.

Sometimes, when I talk about Deliberate Economics today, friends object that it is not possible for *everyone* to live more Deliberately. Maybe: I wasn't thinking about everyone. The chimera taught me to think about my own good first—whatever else I said—and trust that if I did that, everything would work out. *Das Capital,* eh. This sudden concern for everyone takes me by surprise. I was sharing what works with friends whom I see work more to get less. My world is better if my friends improve their finances and health too. We'd have time to celebrate and the food to do it with. Good for me, good for us.

Our animal nature makes some labour necessary to survive, and this labour must result in food and shelter, and arguably exercise, art and culture. We have no choice about that. Deliberate production answers these needs more efficiently than wage slavery, and is more humane. The rest of our choices pertain to our social character, where the chimera works to limit our choices to roles on the work-spend-work wheel, and think this is freedom.

Our wage slavery is maintained by the chimera through an antagonism between ideas, not on a battlefield, or between the handle and the Business-end of a whip. If you can *just choose* that a motorcycle or a cruise will make you happy, you can similarly *just choose* to be even happier with the money, or without debt. From an economic perspective the second choice puts you closer to freedom from wage slavery, and closer to satisfying your nature, and so is in your self-interest. From a planet perspective, a Deliberate life uses less resources than urban life on the wheel, and so permits more of us to survive resource scarcity—if the worry is about what *everyone* can do...

The chimera is looming, requiring a delicate segue around my interlocutor's private battle, and back to something general.

...Always, the denouement of this conversation is a segue to a dystopian future in which social systems fail.

In book and movie plots, the change from middle-class-prosperity to dystopia happens suddenly. Maybe an invasion, a parasite, or a climate disaster. Sometimes it is an economic disaster resulting in a Corporate monopoly, and a society controlled by Business. The fact that it *can* be easier now to acquire basic necessities Deliberately than through social cooperation means that the economy has failed for wage slaves already. Our dystopia started in the past: it's not a prediction about the future. We now expect a biological disaster because the mass extinction is already underway. We don't expect everyone to survive, or to fail all at once. History, like life, is a process, not an event. In a dystopian society, Deliberate Economics rule, because food, shelter and fuel are the capital of choice.

Which brings us back to where we started: a book for those worried about a *future* of low wages, and environmental crises.

There is another way the conversation about Deliberate Economics sometimes ends: the beginning of a Deliberate path to freedom from wage slavery.

The Beginning